Aiki Trading

Trading in Harmony
with the Markets

Aiki Trading

Trading in Harmony
with the Markets

JEFFERY TIE

WILEY

John Wiley & Sons (Asia) Pte. Ltd.

Other Wiley Editorial Offices

John Wiley & Sons, 111 River Street, Hoboken, NJ 07030, USA
John Wiley & Sons, The Atrium, Southern Gate, Chichester, West Sussex, P019 8SQ, United Kingdom
John Wiley & Sons (Canada) Ltd., 5353 Dundas Street West, Suite 400, Toronto, Ontario, M9B 6HB, Canada
John Wiley & Sons Australia Ltd., 42 McDougall Street, Milton, Queensland 4064, Australia
Wiley-VCH, Boschstrasse 12, D-69469 Weinheim, Germany

Library of Congress Cataloging-in-Publication Data
ISBN 978–0–470–82581–5

Typeset in 11/14pt Century-Book by Thomson Digital, India
Printed in Singapore by Toppan Security Printing Pte. Ltd.
10 9 8 7 6 5 4 3 2 1

Contents

Foreword   ix

Preface   xi

Acknowledgments   xiii

Introduction   1

The Philosophy of *Aiki* Trading   2

CHAPTER 1   *Aikido*   7

History   7
The Principles and Techniques of *Aikido*   10

CHAPTER 2   Candlestick Charting   15

Feudal Japan's Ethos, and its Impact on the
   Development of Japanese Candlestick Charting   15
The Methods of *Aiki* Trading   19

CHAPTER 3   The Expanded Sideways Range Pattern   25

Bulls, Bears, and Turtles   28
   Observations and Conclusion   31
Codifying the Trading Rules for the Expanded
   Sideways Range Pattern   31
   The Action Zones   31
   The Entry Trigger   32

Risk and Money Management: The Stop Loss Exit   34
Qualifying the Trade   42

CHAPTER 4   The Directional Trending Pattern   51

Identifying and Trading a Type 1 Trend Pattern   61
Planning the Stop Loss Exit   66
The Structural Risk   68
    The Profit Exit Strategy   68
Timeframe and the Selection of its Relevant
    Moving Average Value   71

CHAPTER 5   The Successful Breakout   77

Managing the Trade   92

CHAPTER 6   Using Oscillators   97

Relative Strength Index   98
The RSI Divergence Signal (or RSI Camouflage Signal) 104
The Slow Stochastic Oscillator   108

**CHAPTER 7   Applying Fibonacci Numbers and Ratios
                in Trade Analysis   119**

Assessing the Fibonacci Profit Target   127

CHAPTER 8   Trade Volume and its Interpretation   139

CHAPTER 9   Risk, Money, and Trade Management   153

The Learning Phase   153
Trading for Profits   155
The Preservation of Capital   156
Money Management: The Preservation of Our Capital   157

**Risk Management Combined with the 2 Percent
Money Management Rule**   158

Position Sizing   161

Winning Trade Management and the Rule of 3   163

CHAPTER 10   On Trading Psychology   **173**

Summary   175

  Beliefs About Success   175

    Market Understanding   175

    **Risk Management, Money Management,
and Trade Management**   176

    Winning Psychology   177

Index   **181**

Foreword

J eff Tie has done me the honor of writing a preface to this book.

Let me state upfront that Jeff is my first friend in Singapore. But as Jeff will tell you, I take pride that I strive to write without fear or favor and this preface is no exception.

I first met Jeff in my first presentation in Singapore and then he attended the first seminar I gave here. Jeff tells me that he had initially dismissed the ideas I presented because what I said went against what he believed then. Jeff took heed of some of my comments—he was open to new ideas even though they went against ingrained habits. That's not to say he adopted the ideas immediately—change that comes easily is seldom worthwhile. In time, he took some of my ideas and made them his own. The result can be seen in this work. I have seen Jeff grow well beyond the seeds that I help planted. He has become a first-class teacher having recently signed a contract to lecture at the Singapore Exchange (SGX) Academy.

The book you are reading presents and reflects Jeff's experience as a trader and teacher. Having read Jeff's book, I believe it deserves a place on your bookshelf and if you are a novice trader, it deserves to be thoroughly studied.

Why should this book be any different from the other hundred or so books on trading success?

Most books focus on one aspect of trading—usually the trading plan. But 30 years in the markets have shown me that trading success comes from the consistent application of a trading plan that has an edge and a risk management plan that controls and manages a trader's risk.

Jeff has done an excellent job on the trading plan and risk-management plan; he has done a competent job on suggesting ways a trader can attain consistent execution. What I like about the book is the way Jeff has taken complex subjects and made them easy to understand. This is no easy task. While I have not tested the plan, I know from experience that it contains all the elements of a robust trading plan with an edge.

On the risk management side, if you take nothing else from the book, take a deep understanding of the risk-expectancy formula. Most newbies crash and burn because they fail to appreciate the importance of this aspect of trading. Jeff did a great job to make a complex subject simple and you should take advantage of the gift on offer.

Ray Barros
Hedge Fund Manager
Author, *The Nature of Trends*
www.tradingsuccess.com/blog
April 2010

Preface

Eastern philosophy extols the cultured individual as one who has a well-rounded education complemented by wide and varied experience. In ancient times this concept, the epitome of the cultured man, was exemplified by the idea that the ideal person would be equally skilled in both the martial arts as well as the literary classics. A more prosaic way of saying this is that the ideal combines both brawn and brain!

This ethos has resonated with me since I first learned about it.

I found "brawn" through the practice of martial arts, and in both *aikido* and *shinkendo* I have found a very high expression of Japanese martial techniques and philosophy. In Japanese, these martial traditions are known as *budo*, meaning the "martial way."

I explored the literary aspect initially through the study of the classical guitar, chess, and eventually in the pursuit of trading competence.

After many years of practice, I have realized that the underlying principles of success in all human endeavors remain constant, be it in either the brawn or the brain category. There is always the requirement to know and understand the technical aspects of our chosen activity, and this can only be achieved through daily, consistent practice. There must also be an innate and burning desire to achieve our vision. This will spark, spur, and drive us onward, especially in the face of difficulty and setback.

I have also come to the realization that there is no end to the learning process. The more we know, the more we realize how little we know. Some may balk at the energy and effort that success requires. However, those who will succeed will need to start some-where. After all, as Lao-tzu, the father of Taoism once wrote, the journey of a thousand miles begins with a single step.

It is my hope that this book will assist you in your search, in your journey and in your quest, for trading competency and eventually trading mastery. I have learned from painful loss, and it is a very humbling experience. I will be very happy if the principles and methods in this book can help you to safely navigate the dangers that abound in the trading arena. Remember, pathfinders know where dangerous quicksand and rocky shoals await the unsuspecting traveler. I will be happy if you treat me as your guide, as your pathfinder in your path and journey to trading competency and trading excellence.

Acknowledgments

I n both martial arts and in trading, I have had the privilege of learning from many different instructors, each of whom have taught me different methods and exposed me to different perspectives.

I specifically wish to acknowledge two special and unique individuals who were, and still are, instrumental in my progress and development.

Lonnie W. Oakes was my martial arts instructor, or *sensei*, who introduced *shinkendo* (Japanese swordsmanship) to me. Lonnie *sensei* taught me the techniques of *shinkendo*, but more importantly, by his own example, he also shared and taught me the martial arts philosophy that I now recognize as essential to success in any life activity. One specific lesson is worth mentioning here. Both Lonnie *sensei* and I were early for class. Lonnie *sensei* started off with a series of basic (but difficult) stretches. Instead of following him, I started a set of sword drills. Lonnie *sensei* stopped me, and pointed out that I was not in the correct body condition to do the sword drills well. I needed to work on improving suppleness and flexibility, which was what Lonnie *sensei* was doing in his basic stretching exercises. He correctly pointed out that I avoided doing what I found to be uncomfortable.

This comment struck a very strong chord in me. I immediately recognized what I needed to do to improve; I needed to work on my weaknesses and by definition, these will be areas that I will naturally dislike, and indeed avoid, because of their inherent difficulty. Lonnie *sensei's* advice, which still resonates with me to this day, is that I must do what I do not like, and then make it normal, and eventually normal will become easy over time. Incremental improvement only occurs this way, and we then need to constantly search for new, difficult hurdles to overcome in order to expand our knowledge and our competencies.

Rei, domo arigato gozaimasu, Lonnie sensei.

In trading, I started off with the widely held fantasy that all I needed was one surefire never-fail technique and all my trades will be forever successful. I searched diligently, and met many more experienced traders, some of whom graciously shared and taught different methods and different perspectives. After years of searching, it is my opinion that there is no such secret technique or Holy Grail that can confer immediate and unfailing success.

I was very fortunate that I eventually met Ray Barros. It was Ray who finally pointed me in the right direction, focusing on the fusion of method, risk management and the mental mindset. In Ray's approach to trading, I recognized the application of the martial arts philosophy, and this in turn strengthened my practice and application of the methods and habits that will eventually lead to trading success. Ray shared with and taught me his methods, but more importantly, Ray taught me to think in terms of probability, and for that I am truly grateful.

Thank you Ray, for being my trading *sensei*.

Nonetheless, Ray will be the first person who will say that all his success is built upon preexisting methods and knowledge, taught by those he learned from. With this in mind, I will also collectively thank all who taught and influenced both Lonnie *sensei* and Ray, for without them, I too would probably not have traveled this path, nor arrived at this stage of my journey. Specifically, I wish to acknowledge Toshishiro Obata *sensei*, the founder of *shinkendo*, and J. Peter Steidlmayer, who codified the rules of the Market Profile.

Thank you, Obata *sensei*, and Steidlmayer *sensei*, for teaching the instructors who eventually guided me.

I have had the privilege of teaching with the Singapore Exchange and also with the International Shinkendo Federation.

My understanding of martial arts and of trading has improved because of the teaching that I have done.

The line drawings in this book were the work of my *shinkendo* students, Deepak Ram Ayengar and Yong Jie Yu. You did a fantastic job with finesse and skill. These beautiful visuals will help in the understanding of the martial arts concepts that can be also applied to trading. I am deeply grateful to both of you.

It is my hope that you, the reader will benefit from this work. I humbly thank all who have studied, or will study with me in the future; you deserve my thanks as well for helping me improve.

I wish also to thank Grace Pundyk, who as editor in charge of this project, provided invaluable help and suggestions that improved the flow and presentation of the content, for which I am deeply grateful.

I also acknowledge the contribution of my family. You have all stood by me through turbulent times and difficult circumstances. Thank you, Kerry, Algernon, and Anastasia.

Finally, all mistakes in the book are solely mine.

Disclaimer: All charts in this book are drawn with the Market Analyst 6 charting software, and are gratefully used with the expressed permission of Market Analyst where noted.

The DealBook® 360 screen captures were used with permission from GFT. GFT and John Wiley & Sons (Asia) are separate and independent companies. GFT's DealBook® 360 trading software is offered as a free service to GFT's customers. However, GFT is not responsible for the information provided in this book for which John Wiley & Sons (Asia) is solely responsible. Forex trading presents substantial risk of loss with or without the use of GFT's DealBook® 360 trading software.

Introduction

This book is written for the serious beginner who is searching for a basic primer in understanding market behavior and applying this knowledge to trade in the financial markets. The concepts covered in this book are based on the foundational course that I conduct for SGX Academy.

It is important that I clearly state what this book will and will *not* achieve, so that you, dear readers, can decide whether this is what you need and desire. Perhaps an analogy here will illustrate what I mean.

In the learning of Japanese martial arts, the beginner student is usually taught one basic technique. The student learns and internalizes this single basic technique so that he can respond to a specific combat situation. If this combat situation is altered, then the initial technique may not provide the student with a satisfactory solution. He needs to learn new techniques and then internalize them with his existing knowledge in order to widen the combat situations that he understands and can properly respond to.

So it is with trading, and my approach to teaching and learning trading techniques. Financial markets are complex, and the way the markets can behave is also complex. It will be extremely difficult, if not impossible, for any beginner to gain immediate mastery of complex market behavior. The logical solution is to break down the complexities into bite-size basic building blocks. As the student progresses, additional knowledge is acquired and existing knowledge built upon, allowing the student to begin understanding ever more complex situations.

Obviously, the path to mastery (in both martial arts and trading) will be paved with hard work and sacrifice. Many will start, but only the determined few will eventually succeed. So if you are looking for instant success or if you believe that the mastery of trading is easy, then this book is probably not for you.

THE PHILOSOPHY OF *AIKI* TRADING

This book links trading in the financial markets to the principles and philosophy of *aiki*, which means "harmony" in Japanese. Aikido is the martial art that best exemplifies the concept of *aiki*. The life philosophy as expressed through *aikido*, and indeed through any other martial art, also promotes core values and molds the character of its proponents. Discipline, tenacity, focus, and commitment are but a few of these values and characteristics that the dedicated martial arts student will build and nurture. These are also some of the same values and characteristics that are essential for success in any other life endeavors, including trading in financial markets.

After many years of practice in both Japanese martial arts and in trading the financial markets, I have noticed great similarities between the principles and philosophy of the two.

On the surface, the casual observer may say that both disciplines are diametrically different. However, long-term practitioners acknowledge the many commonalities.

Richard McCall, in his book *The Way of the Warrior Trader*, published by John Wiley & Sons, encapsulated these similarities in his ACTION acronym. I have adopted and amended this acronym to reflect the principles by which I believe the successful martial artist and the successful trader should live by.

A FOR ACCEPTANCE

The martial artist must accept that his path to mastery will involve discomfort and even pain in the *dojo* (training hall). The

---

aspiring trader must accept that both loss and profit are the only outcomes in the uncertain arena of trading and that financial pain and pleasure will be part and parcel of his learning experience. Both the martial artist and the trader have accepted that the path to mastery will require commitment of time, effort, energy, and resources. Chinese *wushu* practitioners will recognize the same concepts in their term, "eating bitter."

C for Calmness and Clarity

Calmness and clarity are qualities that all martial arts practitioners strive to achieve. The calm warrior will be able to meet the challenges of strife and combat with a clear mind. A clear, calm mind allows the martial artist to move with trained reflex responses in the face of danger. Similarly, the trader whose mind is calm and clear will be better prepared to correctly respond to the emotional dangers that the financial markets are well known for. Greed, hope, fear, and despair have devastated many traders in the past and will continue to devastate many aspiring traders in the future. Successful traders must meet these four apocalyptic horsemen with calmness and clarity in mind, spirit, and action.

T for Trust in Training

The martial artist has trust that his training will produce the correct winning response in combat. Similarly, the aspiring trader who perserveres in his practice of a good trading method will eventually gain confidence, and will trust in his abilities through disciplined training.

I for Imagination

Every successful person in *any* endeavor must have belief in their eventual success. Belief must first start as imagination. The successful martial artist or trader must combine both dedicated disciplined effort with specific visualization through the imagination of what success will be like for him. *Cogito, ergo sum* (Latin for "I think, therefore I am") will be the mental spur for any successful person.

O FOR ONLY

I was training with my *shinkendo* sword instructor Lonnie *sensei*. We were practicing contact sparring with wooden *bokken*. *Sensei*'s attack was fast, and my mind and body were not able to correctly respond in time to his strikes. *Sensei* admonished me. "Don't live in the past. It is over, so forget it." Facing him again, I next tried to anticipate his attack. But instead of blocking where I thought his attack would be, I was hit by an unexpected strike. *Sensei* again admonished me. "Don't live in the future, it has not happened yet! Only live in the now." For the aspiring trader, "Only live in the now" is a good mantra. Living in the bitterness of prior losses or living upon past glories will never lead to the mindset changes that success will require of us. Living exclusively in the future at the expense of the present will also be detrimental to one's success. We need to learn from the past, and correctly imagine the future, but not at the expense of the present.

This is of particular importance to a trader. When the market goes against the original hoped for result, many traders live in the past and continue to pray that their desired result can still occur, and ignore what is actually happening in reality. Then, there are also occasions when the trader tries to anticipate what the market can do, effectively "living in the future" instead of waiting for his method to activate and trigger the trade, which is the "living in the now" entry. They then find that they have entered a trade in anticipation, but soon discover that the proper signal did not actually occur yet!

N FOR NEVER

The *samurai* ethos is one in which the warrior is always prepared to face his own mortality, his own death. This did not mean that the *samurai* were morbid or morose. On the contrary, the *samurai* embraced life and lived life well. But in order to face death, a *samurai* had to live life without regrets. The creed was to never look back once action had started; so too for the trader. Once in a trade, he must never look back with or at the regrets of the past.

The trading principles of the *aiki* trader require the practitioner to understand the nature of market behavior, and to act in harmony with the market.

In a continuing uptrend, my preferred form of *aiki* trading will buy the corrective dip. The *aiki* trader enters and attacks the weak seller at the correction's end, and is entering in harmony with the major uptrend. Similarly, in a continuing downtrend, the *aiki* trader will sell the corrective rally.

In a continuing sideways or range bound market, the *aiki* trader will buy the floor and sell the ceiling precisely because he recognizes that the selling force weakens at the support, and buying forces weaken at the resistance. This will allow him an attacking entry directly into the weakening force.

The principles of *aiki* trading will require the trader to competently execute his trading plan, which must be based on a solid understanding of *kihon*, or "basic fundamentals," of market behavior. In other words, success in trading, indeed in any life endeavor requires the practitioner to:

1. Know what to do;
2. Do what you know; and
3. Do it flawlessly.

Remember, there is no "silver bullet" or "secret manual" or "Holy Grail" that confers immediate success. Only determination and the correct practice of a robust method can lead to eventual mastery and success.

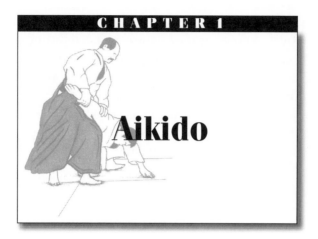

CHAPTER 1

Aikido

HISTORY

Modern day *aikido* has its roots in the martial traditions of ancient Japan going back to antiquity. There is no official written documentation that can trace *aikido* back to its root art. Nonetheless, it is generally acknowledged that the history of *aikido* has been handed down orally to present-day headmasters. The version of *aikido* presented in this chapter is sourced with permission from the International Shinkendo Federation and follows the oral tradition closely.

Yoshimitsu Miyamoto and his brother Yoshiie, who lived in Japan in the 12th century, were both famous *samurai* and claimed descent from Emperor Seiwa (858–876 AD). The Miyamoto family name had been conferred by Japanese emperors on sons that were non-heirs to the throne.

In order to improve their martial skills, the brothers researched the science and working mechanics of the human body and its skeletal functions. They did this by dissecting the bodies of criminals and those who died in the numerous civil wars of that period. Armed with this knowledge and understanding, they devised and formatted some techniques that they then applied in combat. These techniques were collectively known as *daito* after their family ancestral home, the *Daitokan*. The brothers taught these techniques to members of the family and eventually, by the 15th century, one branch of the family established itself in a province known as Takeda Kai. This family branch then adopted Takeda as their family name.

During the era of almost constant civil warfare and strife, survival depended on mastery of martial skill and techniques, which had to be combat effective. The Japanese term for martial techniques is *jutsu*, a technique that had to be utilitarian and effectively deadly. There was very little philosophical thought or notions of spirit and character polishing, especially when the victors of combat lived and the wages of defeat was death. However, as time and civil society progressed, martial techniques were used less for combat and more for polishing the character and spirit.

Originally, it is said that *aikido*'s root art was developed as a combat art based primarily on sword and spear techniques. Such techniques were used on battlefields against other soldiers wearing armor. At the time, empty-hand combat was practiced as a secondary study to the weapons arts. Subsumed within this type of empty-hand combat technique were additional levels of training known as *aikijutsu*. Research suggests that *aiki* was added to *jutsu* to reflect the change from the martial art being primarily sword-based to an art more focused on unarmed combat techniques. The basic, more generic empty hand *jujutsu*, or *jujitsu*, techniques could be used offensively, while the *aikijutsu* was more defensive in its nature and application. *Aikijutsu* was reserved for the higher-ranking *samurai*. The techniques continued to evolve and adapt with the needs of the times and were transmitted eventually to the Takeda family in the 16th century as *gotenjutsu*, or martial arts, for use inside a palace. It is interesting to note that for security reasons, the use of weapons within the palace was prohibited; so empty-hand combat techniques were extensively used in such security-conscious locations.

Kunitsugu Takeda, the sword instructor of the Aizu clan, passed on these teachings to qualified members within the clan. Top retainers, lords, and generals from Aizu, learned *aikijutsu* as a defensive art to be used while working within the Edo castle, which was the seat of the Tokogawa Shogunate, Japan's military government of the day. As time passed, the Takeda family's martial traditions in the Meiji period (late 19th century) become known eventually as *daito-ryu aikijutsu.*

Sogaku Takeda lived in the Meiji era (1868–1912). During this time, major changes were occurring throughout Japanese society. Feudal Japan was forcibly dragged into the Industrial Age, and the process involved the assimilation of industrialized Western ways, the adoption of international trade agreements, as well as the elimination of Japanese society's social caste and class structure. The objective was to very quickly develop Japan as an industrial and colonial power, equal to the existing Western colonial powers of the day.

To achieve this goal, society and social mores had to be drastically changed. One such change made during the Meiji Restoration was, in 1876, a ban on the wearing of swords in public. This deeply affected the previously ruling *samurai* class, and was deemed as a slap in their collective face, because the wearing of swords in public was the hereditary right of the *samurai* class. Seeing the effects of these new changes, Sogaku modified the emphasis of *daito-ryu aikijutsu* from an art form exclusive to the ruling classes to one available to all. As a result of these changes, the revised art of *daito-ryu aikijutsu* became very popular. Sogaku is now acknowledged as its reviver.

Sogaku taught and nurtured several outstanding martial artists during his life. A very talented and accomplished student was Morihei Ueshiba, who eventually founded modern-day *aikido*.

Morihei trained and taught *daito-ryu aikijutsu* diligently during the years prior to World War Two (the pre-war period), while at the same time beginning development of his *aikido* style.

Immediately after the war ended, there was a general institutional repudiation of the martial and warlike aspects of Japanese society. Eventually, however, after the healing of the immediate post-war years, the ban on martial arts and traditions was lifted and Morihei resumed teaching *aikido*, which he then continuously modified and refined until his death in 1969.

Morihei's *aikido* evolved from its more combative *daito-ryu aikijutsu* ancestor, in both its techniques and its philosophy. In

Japanese, *do* is the term that describes this "way of life." The *jutsu* philosophy seeks to achieve decisive victory by utterly defeating the opponent, and if victory calls for a fatal resolution, then so be it. The softer gentler *aikido* philosophy, however and seeks to also achieve a decisive victory, by demonstrating decisive, superior technical ability and accurate timing in order to gain control over the opponent. Once the opponent realizes the futility of further conflict, the aikido-ka will then voluntarily release his opponent, and both will leave the scene of conflict alive and intact.

THE PRINCIPLES AND TECHNIQUES OF *AIKIDO*

Early Eastern philosophers pondering the nature of life and the universe observed that there is a duality in how everything works and operates. This duality is symbolized by the yin-yang symbol: light and darkness; strength and weakness; white and black; and life and death are all very common examples of what is represented by this symbol. Such thinking and philosophy also found expression in the understanding and the techniques of the martial arts.

In *aikido*, this core belief can be expressed thus:

1. Attack strongly if your enemy is weak; in other words, be hard if your opponent is soft.
2. Harmonize and merge with your enemy if he is strong; therefore, be soft if your opponent is hard.

The key to success in *aikido* is to understand the state of the opponent. The competent *aikido-ka*, by virtue of dedicated practice and superior technical ability, is able to correctly gauge whether his opponent is weak or is strong, and whether the opponent is balanced, or is off balance. Only then can he select the correct technique and response in order to resolve the danger in a harmonious manner.

The following illustrations "Controlling the weak force," show one basic technique that demonstrates how a weak opponent can be

Controlling the weak force
Illustration by Deepak Ram Ayengar and Yong Jie Yu.

controlled, by competently assessing that the opponent is weak, and then directly entering, turning, and diverting the weak opponent away from his original path.

Let us now try to visualize how this *aikido* technique can be used and applied in trading. If the competent *aiki* trader, by virtue of dedicated practice, superior technical ability, and good timing, is able to determine that the selling force is weak, then he needs to join with the strong buying force by directly opposing and entering against the weak seller, turning and diverting and reversing the weak seller's direction. Conversely, and also obviously, if the competent *aiki* trader is able to determine that the buying force is weak, then he can join the strong selling force, to repel and reverse the direction of the weak buyer.

Now we look at "Be with the strong force."

Here, a strong opponent is charging in. The *aikido-ka* assesses this force as strong and unstoppable, but by virtue of dedicated practice, superior technical ability and good timing, is able to harmonize and merge with this strong force. In trading terms, if the competent trader accesses that the market is strongly bullish and up, he will be looking for ways and means to merge and buy, instead of selling in opposition to the strong force. Similarly, in a strong bearish market, it will be wise to merge with the selling force, and not act in opposition as a buyer.

These two *aikido* examples will be used as a mental anchor in a visualization process that will guide the thinking and action of the competent trader using *aiki* principles. We will be referencing these images to reinforce the *aiki* trading concepts that will appear throughout the rest of this book.

Be with the strong force
Illustration by Deepak Ram Ayengar and Yong Jie Yu.

CHAPTER 2

Candlestick Charting

FEUDAL JAPAN'S ETHOS, AND ITS IMPACT ON THE DEVELOPMENT OF JAPANESE CANDLESTICK CHARTING

History shows that we, as a species, are combative and war-like in nature. Certainly, the Japanese were no different from any other race, with their history replete with conflicts between clans, regions, and warlords. However, their ability to link their methods and ways of war to the methods and ways of trading have contributed to the knowledge and ethos of trading today.

Arguably, the crescendo of feudal Japanese civil conflict was the *Sengoku jidai*, or the "warring period," which lasted for 100 years. During this period, between the 16th and 17th centuries, *daimyo*, or warlords, waged constant civil war in the contest for prestige, power and political supremacy. James Clavell popularized this period with his bestseller, *Shogun*, which is a fictionalized adaptation of the events occurring during the climax of the *Sengoku jidai* epoch.

Oda Nobunaga was the *daimyo* who nearly achieved total supremacy. Unfortunately for Nobunaga, Mitsuhide Akechi, one of Nobunaga's own generals, successfully schemed to have him removed from power. However, Mitsuhide's attempt to seize control and power was futile. Nobunaga's two foremost generals, Hedeyoshi Toyotomi and Ieyasu Tokugawa, rallied the rest of the Nobunaga forces and prevailed over Mitsuhide. Although Ieyasu was nominally subservient to Hedeyoshi, the reality was more of a bipolar political situation, fraught with tension and intrigue.

Collectively, the three men, Nobunaga, Hideyoshi, and Ieyasu, were known as the unifiers of Japan. Nobunaga was the one who probably did most of the unification work, through both diplomacy and combat, while Hedeyoshi and Ieyasu were the ones to consolidate Nobunaga's efforts. It is therefore often said: "Nobunaga planted the rice; Hedeyoshi harvested and cooked it; but Ieyasu ate it.

Nobunaga Oda
Illustration by Deepak Ram Ayengar and Yong Jie Yu.

Ieyasu Tokugawa
Illustration by Deepak Ram Ayengar and Yong Jie Yu.

It was during the reign of Hedeyoshi Toyotomi that the port city of Osaka became Japan's economic center. Its seaport and its road connectivity made it ideal as a commercial and logistics center.

By virtue of its logistics capabilities, Osaka quickly became Japan's largest trade and financial center. During this period, people were divided into five castes; *samurai*, farmer, artisan, merchant, and *eta*, or the "untouchables."

The military government was comprised mainly of the *samurai* caste, who treated merchants with disdain. One such merchant was Keian Yodoya, whose business was in the warehousing, transportation, and trading of rice. He was so successful that his front yard became Japan's first rice exchange. The envious government of the day confiscated Keian's fortune on the excuse that the merchant was obscenely richer than the *samurai* caste. This state of affairs, of taxing and intimidating the merchants, inhibited the development of

the economy. It wasn't until Ieyasu Tokugawa defeated the Toyotomi faction and assumed full political power that Japanese society
stabilized and new economic opportunities emerged.

As the Japanese economy was still based on rice, candlestick
charting was increasingly used to track the performance of rice
prices that were traded on the now institutionalized market that had
become known as the Dojima Rice Exchange.

The Dojima Rice Exchange was established in the late 1600s.
After 1710, rice trading included both the trading of physical rice as
well as rice warehouse receipts. These became known as rice
coupons, and were essentially what we now consider to be futures
contracts. Therefore, the Osaka rice brokerage and trading business
became the foundation for the city's wealth. Rice became the
medium of exchange. The Japanese currency unit, the *koku*, was
a measurement of the amount of rice required to feed one *samurai*
for one year.

A *daimyo* in need of money could send his surplus rice, or even
his future rice harvests to the Osaka brokers in exchange for a rice
coupon. This coupon could then be sold. Many *daimyo* conveniently
alleviated their cashflow problems by this method. Unwisely, sometimes many years of future expected harvests were forward sold to
take care of current expenses. "Spend today what you can earn
tomorrow!" seems to be the recurring mantra of all times.

With the rice coupon becoming an actively traded entity, the
Dojima Rice Exchange became the world's first futures exchange.
Rice coupons were like futures contracts, as compared to the
underlying physical rice. It is said that over the same accounting
period, the trading volume of rice futures was about four times the
volume of the entire stock of rice in the country.

It was during this period that candlestick trading became more
refined. Munehisa Honma, the youngest son of the Honma family,
inherited the family's trading business due to his extraordinary
trading savvy.

Munehisa research explains the impact of the underlying psychology that motivates all who trade in the rice market. Honma's
method to display price activity eventually became known as

"candlesticks." His research and findings, frequently referred to as the *"Sakata* rules," became the framework for Japanese investment philosophy.

Japanese candlestick analysis was not widely known only because of the language barrier. It was unknown in the West, which developed its own methodology in bar charts, which also explains the psychological motivation of market participants.

In 1986, Shimizu Seiki's *The Japanese Chart of Charts* was the first book about Japanese candlesticks to be published in the English language. But it was arguably Steve Nison who popularized and promoted the interest in candlestick analysis to the general investing public in the United States. Steve Nison's initial publication *Japanese Candlestick Charting Techniques* was published in 1991, six years after Shimizu's book. All of us who use Japanese candlesticks in our trading acknowledge with deep gratitude both Shimizu Seiki for "planting the rice" by introducing Japanese candlestick charting to the Western investment world, and Steve Nison for "kneading the dough" with his dedication, and his continuing effort to widen, promote and popularize Japanese candlestick charting methods and philosophy.

THE METHODS OF *AIKI* TRADING

There is a very famous quote from Sun Tzu's *The Art of War*:

> *So it is said that if you know your enemies and know yourself, you can win a thousand battles without a single loss.*
>
> *If you only know your opponent, but not yourself, you may win or may lose.*
>
> *If you know neither yourself nor your enemy, you will always endanger yourself.*

In trading, success is dependent on the correct selection of the correct strategy. The correct strategy is, in turn, determined by how well you understand the behavior of the market. In other words, this is the "know your opponent" requirement of success. This is one of the three crucial pillars of trading success. I call this aspect of trading success "market understanding."

At its most basic level, every market fluctuates because of changes in supply and demand. The emotional factors of greed, hope, fear, and despair affect all market participants and, in turn, also affect perception of market value.

If traders perceive that the market is undervalued, then these traders will tend to buy, and their buying action results in increased demand. Conversely, if traders perceive that the market is over-valued, then these traders will tend to sell, and their selling action results in increased supply.

Candlestick charting is one basic way to visually represent the changes in supply and demand within a specified period. The opening price is the price at which both combatants (buyer and seller) agree on value (the contact of swords). The combatants (buyer and seller) will advance and retreat during the period of combat, and the distance gained by one of the combatants at the end of this period will represent the strength of the winner (the candle-stick body), and the total distance the combatants traversed is displayed as the "candlestick wicks," also known as "shadows."

Using this imagery, we can visualize strong winning forces eventually pushing back the weak losing forces. A directional candle opens within 25 percent of one extreme and closes within 25 percent of the other extreme. To illustrate, let us assume that the opening transaction of the day was recorded at 110.25 (or lower), and the last transaction of the day was recorded at 110.75 (or higher). During the day, the market traded to a low of 110.00 and to a high of 111.00. By our definition, this was a directional bull candle with the market opening within 25 percent of the day's low, and closing within 25 percent of the day's high. This is a very important concept that we will be using throughout this book (Figure 2.1).

Conversely, if the market traded to the same high of 111.00 and also the same low of 110.00, but opened at 110.75 (or higher) and

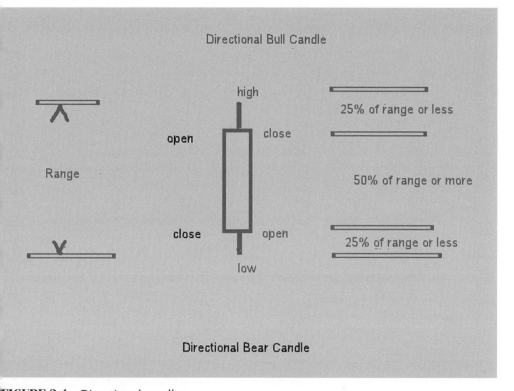

FIGURE 2.1 Directional candles
Source: Reproduced by permission of *Market Analyst*.

closed at 110.25 (or lower), then the candlestick is described as a directional bear candle.

In looking at candlestick charts, we observe that although individual candles can be random, collectively there is some pattern and order in how markets behave, as Figure 2.2 illustrates.

In a directional trend, the market moves in some form of expansion and contraction pattern. The expansion move is called an impulse, and in a directional uptrend this impulse is pointing upward. Conversely, in a directional downtrend, this impulse will point downward. The contraction move is known as a correction. In a directional uptrend, the impulse peaks and the correction lows tend to be higher, and in a directional downtrend, these impulse lows

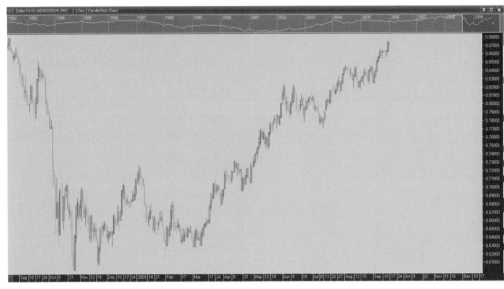

FIGURE 2.2   Pattern and order
Source: Reproduced by permission of *Market Analyst.*

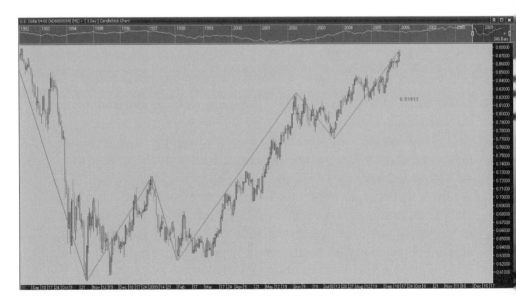

FIGURE 2.3   Expansion and contraction pattern
Source: Reproduced by permission of *Market Analyst.*

and correction highs tend to be lower. There is a key difference between the impulse and the correction; note that impulses are significantly larger than corrections, as Figure 2.3 illustrates.

In a sideways or range bound pattern, the market establishes supports and resistances. This is a very important component of market understanding, and we will begin our study of market behavior with the next chapter dedicated to the sideways or range bound pattern.

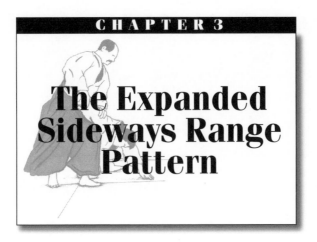

CHAPTER 3

The Expanded Sideways Range Pattern

The sideways range pattern is relatively easy to understand if we study the emotional forces that govern the actions of market participants. We start off with the premise that at perceived undervalued prices, buyers emerge. The resulting action of these buyers will propel the market to perceived overvalued prices, where sellers emerge. Selling forces then push prices down.

In a sideways range pattern, the market forms a roughly horizontal support as well as a roughly horizontal resistance. Figure 3.1 illustrates this.

Let us assume that we initiated a sell trade at A and when the market dropped to B, we exited our sale with a profitable buy, and also initiated a new buy trade at B. Now let us imagine our feelings with that of the initial selling trade at A. As this turns out to be a profitable trade, our minds will associate this profit with feelings of pleasure, especially when we exited at B, and the profit is realized.

Now let us assume that instead of initiating a sell trade, we bought at A. How would we feel as the market drops toward B? At

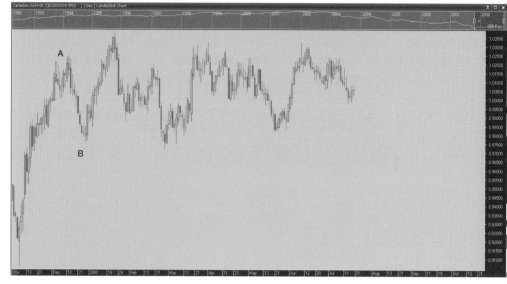

FIGURE 3.1 Sideways pattern
Source: Reproduced by permission of *Market Analyst.*

the least, we will feel a sense of frustration, and even anger, with ourselves and possibly with the market for frustrating and conspiring against us! As the market continues to drop, we will feel financial loss and this loss is associated with pain. We will probably be hoping that the market can recover so that our loss will be minimized. We may even promise the gods of fortune that we will exit if the market can move back to our break-even level. This is because at our break-even level, the pain will be removed, and we will feel relief from the frustration and pain of a bad trade.

The principle to remember is that the human psyche will gravitate toward pleasure, and will shy away from pain. As the market recovers from the B low, it will move closer to the A high. When the market eventually approaches the A high, the emotional memories that are associated with the A high will start to work upon the minds of the market participants. Those who have previously experienced pleasure at A will tend to take the same action that resulted in such pleasure, so this happy group will tend to act as sellers. Those who previously bought at A will have painful memories and their new action will most likely be opposite to what they did originally, so instead of buying, this group will most likely be selling.

There will also be a group of market participants who did not sell at A, and could only observe with regret as the market dropped to B. This group is likely to sell when the market makes the subsequent attempt to approach A, as they would want to capture the pleasure that they missed before.

In this example, A represents what is called the ceiling or resistance that tends to cap the upward move.

Using the same principles, we can also infer that future downward attempts from the ceiling will be met with buyers who have pleasurable memories at B. The sellers who first sold at B and have memories of pain, will therefore now reverse their original action and will buy. Also, those who were passive observers before will now be new potential buyers who no longer wish to miss out on the perceived potential for profit and pleasure.

In this example, B represents what is called the floor or support that tends to limit the downside move.

We will now consider the three variations of the sideways range pattern. The first variation can be known as the 100 percent perfect sideways range whereby after establishing the ceiling and floor, the market then proceeds to trade to the *exact* resistance and the *exact* support (Figure 3.2).

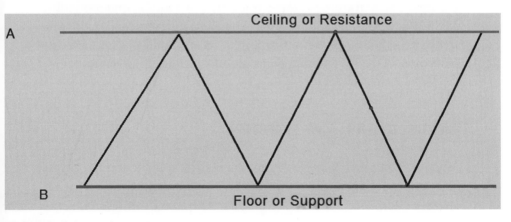

FIGURE 3.2 Perfect sideways variation
Source: Reproduced by permission of *Market Analyst.*

Logic and experience will tell us that although the perfect sideways range market may sometimes occur, this is rather unlikely to occur frequently precisely because we live and trade in an imperfect world. What is more probable is that the ceiling and floor may shift. At times, the market may almost reach, but does not penetrate the support or resistance, and at times it may overshoot and expand the original support and resistance and then revert into the sideways range pattern (Figure 3.3).

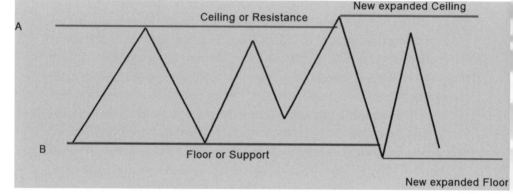

FIGURE 3.3 Imperfect sideways variations
Source: Reproduced by permission of *Market Analyst.*

It is crucial for the beginner trader to have a solid understanding of the sideways range mode. This is because markets tend to operate in a corrective mode more often than in an impulse mode and the sideways range is one important manifestation of correction.

BULLS, BEARS, AND TURTLES

Most market participants are familiar with the bulls and the bears. The bull represents buying forces and buyers, and the bear represents selling forces and sellers. However, most traders may not know of the turtle.

Jack Schwager, in his excellent book, *Market Wizards*, interviewed a group of super-traders collectively known as the "turtles." These turtle traders were trained by Dennis Conner and William Eckhardt. Their objective was to prove or refute the proposition that successful traders can be trained to succeed, and that the successful trader need not be naturally gifted. The result of this experiment proved that nurture can indeed overcome the limitation of nature, and that traders can be successfully trained to excel. The fact that we can all be trained is good news for all beginner traders!

Turtle traders essentially ride on trends and have recorded consistently high returns over long periods. One of the entry rules used by the turtles was to buy a new 20-day high (or sell a new 20-day low). However, Laurence A. Conner and Linda Bradford Raschke, in their book *Street Smarts*, analyzed the turtle's trade statistics and found that the turtle path to profits was paved with significant drawdowns. This was due to the essential nature of the turtle trend trading method, which requires trading on breakouts. However, the attempt to break out of a sideways range, or band, has a statistical failure rate of 70 percent. This statistic implies that the turtle traders would have a 70 percent chance of being stopped out of any given trade signal. Their overall success depends on a significantly higher average dollar win when their method produces the 30 percent winning trades. The total profits thus generated by the 30 percent hit rate would then compensate for and significantly exceed the losses generated by the 70 percent miss rate.

Conner and Bradford Raschke devised a method to profit from the times the turtles will be wrong. They called their method "Turtle Soup" in jest, as they hoped to profit from the times the turtles lost, in other words, making soup out of turtles! Essentially, the Turtle Soup method is to wait for the sideways range to expand, and thereafter revert to the sideways range. Put another way, the attempt to break out of the sideways range is either successful and the market embarks on a directional impulse and trend (turtle wins, Figure 3.4) or the attempt fails (turtles become soup, Figure 3.5).

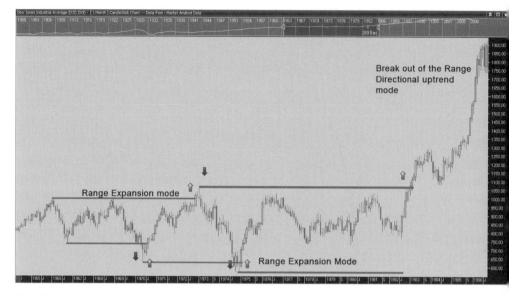

FIGURE 3.4 Successful breakout
Source: Reproduced by permission of *Market Analyst.*

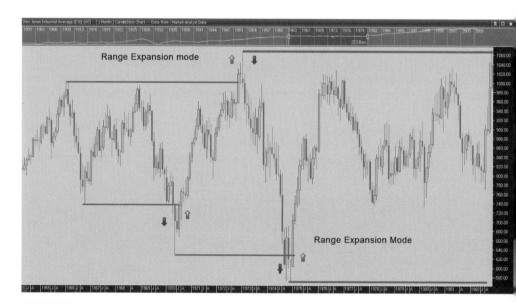

FIGURE 3.5 Failed breakout
Source: Reproduced by permission of *Market Analyst.*

We can begin to see and appreciate this sideways range expansion pattern. What do we observe? More importantly, can this pattern be traded? Can we codify a set of rules to define the sideways range trading strategy?

Observations and Conclusion

When the range expands, the turtle's trade statistics suggest that there is a 70 percent chance that the market can revert into the sideways range.

Should the breakout attempt fail, and the market is indeed in the expanded sideways range, we can then expect that the market has a high probability of traveling to the opposite side of the sideways range. We can also expect that as long as the range mode is intact, the market will tend to travel from ceiling to floor and from floor to ceiling.

We can therefore conclude that this pattern is a viable pattern that can be traded. It is also a very robust pattern because this pattern is based on the psyche of traders, who will tend to gravitate toward pleasure and to avoid pain. We will therefore define a trade plan with an entry and exit method that trades specifically when the market is in the expanded sideways range pattern.

CODIFYING THE TRADING RULES FOR THE EXPANDED SIDEWAYS RANGE PATTERN

The Action Zones

The first rule is to define the current sideways range. The action area is only near the ceiling or the floor of the sideways range. We will need to identify the "mountain peaks" and "valley bottoms" in our chart. If the market is trading near a valley low, then we are looking to buy once the range expands and then fails to continue down. In Figure 3.6, the market is trading near a valley low. The valley low is

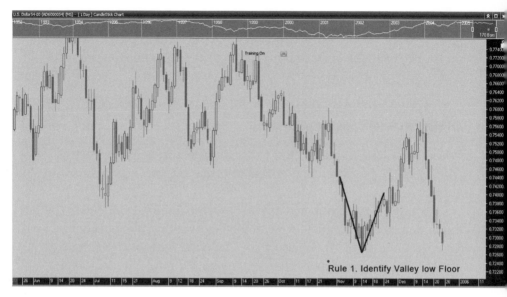

FIGURE 3.6 Valley bottom
Source: Reproduced by permission of *Market Analyst.*

defined as a lowest bar with at least eight higher candles on both the right and the left of the valley candle, with a total look back period of 55 candles. This will clearly define the period in which we expect the sideways range pattern to occur.

The Entry Trigger

The second rule is to project a horizontal line from this valley to the right of the chart. This projected line will define the current sideways floor. It will also visually show any attempted breakout, and also act as a trigger to indicate if the market is reverting into a sideways range (see Figure 3.7).

The third rule is to wait for the breakout. In this case the market has to trade to a new low that is lower than the current valley.

The scenario as shown in Figure 3.8 now has two possibilities. Either the turtles will be correct and the market collapses, or the turtles are wrong and the range expands.

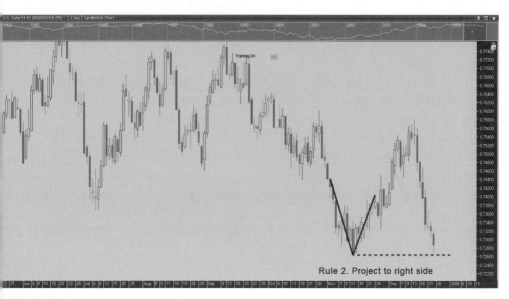

FIGURE 3.7 Define the entry trigger
Source: Reproduced by permission of *Market Analyst*.

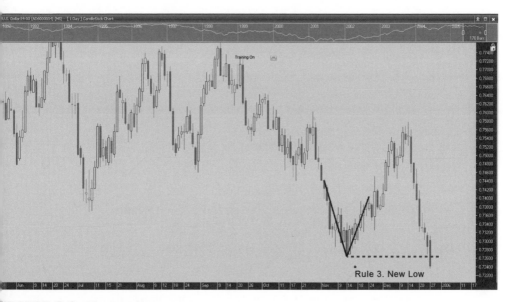

FIGURE 3.8 The breakout event
Source: Reproduced by permission of *Market Analyst*.

The market will need to close *above* the previous valley (marked by the dotted line) if the range expansion scenario is more likely to occur.

The *aiki* trader, like his martial counterpart, has not yet entered combat, but is in the state of focused awareness, and is constantly assessing the market for a trading opportunity.

The fourth rule is to buy if the market closes above the dotted line trigger. Figure 3.9 illustrates the candle that triggers the buy action.

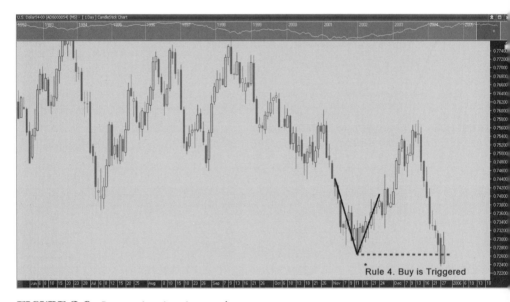

FIGURE 3.9 Buy action is triggered
Source: Reproduced by permission of *Market Analyst.*

The *aiki* trader, like his martial counterpart, acts decisively and without hesitation once the entry signal is recognized.

Risk and Money Management: The Stop Loss Exit

The fifth rule is to determine a trading stop loss. This is a very important concept that is mandatory for all traders to understand and internalize. The risk management aspect is the second pillar of successful trading because it can ensure our long-term survival. Whenever we enter any given trade, we are never certain whether the trade will succeed or fail. We must observe past actions for patterns that we deem to be reliable, and trade these patterns as they occur. The market will then move either in our favor or against us, and will either reward us with a profit, or punish us with a loss. It is critical for our own long-term survival that any single loss we suffer is not a career-ending loss. Let me quote John Hayden, who wrote *The 21 Irrefutable Truths about Trading,* in which he states that over time, 95 percent of traders fail, and that only 5 percent of traders succeed. The reason this occurs is again explained by the nature of the human psyche: we tend to gravitate towards pleasure and away from pain. In trading, pleasure is represented by profit, so the moment most traders have a profit, there is overwhelming psychological pressure to take the profit and realize the pleasure immediately. There is also a concurrent fear that if the profit is not realized, then the profit may turn into a loss, and pleasure can change into pain. Most traders succumb to this psychological pressure and as a result, whenever their trades are positive, profits are relatively small. However, when their trades are negative, the psychological pressure is to avoid the loss, by hoping that the loss can reverse and that the pain can become pleasure instead. Yes, sometimes this hope is realized, but more often than not, the market moves against the trader and the loss starts to grow, together with the pain of the increasing loss. Eventually, the trader exits when the pain is just too much to bear, and this is usually accompanied by a feeling of utter despair. We can see how and why the vast majority of traders fail. They fail because their overall losses are larger than their overall profits. Successful traders are prepared to delay their pleasure and will accept their pain quickly, precisely because they understand that their profits have to be relatively larger than their losses. Therefore, every good trade must incorporate a method to minimize loss and to maximize profit. The tool that we will use to set our loss is the Average True Range (ATR). This is a statistical calculation of the true range over a fixed period. We will define our ATR time period over a 60-candle time span (see Figure 3.10).

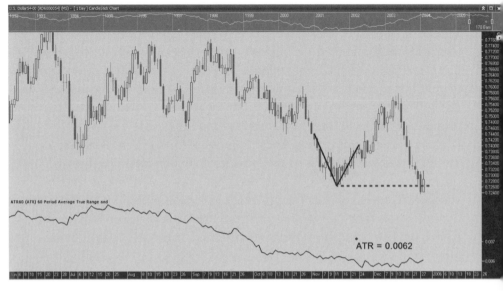

FIGURE 3.10 Average true range
Source: Reproduced by permission of *Market Analyst.*

Rule # 6

  Think of the ATR as a filter. We will be prepared to accept the
risk and the pain of any move against us as long as the move is
defined by the ATR. If the market moves against us by more than the
ATR, then we will assume that the market is no longer in an extended
range, but more likely to be in a directional trend. In our example, we
will identify the new low, and filter the ATR below this low. We will
now be able to define where we will exit if the market trades against
us. In our example, the trade is to go long (buy) so the loss has to be
set below the entry. The formula is:

$$\text{Stop Loss} = \text{New Low} - \text{ATR}.$$

In Figure 3.11, Stop Loss $= 0.7236 - 0.0062 = 0.7174$

  Using the imagery of *aikido*, we have assessed that the seller is
weak, and we have now entered directly as a buyer. The stop loss that
we have planned is equivalent to the *aikido* practitioner acknowl-
edging that the weak attacker (the seller) has concealed his strength
if he can re-exert his force in his original direction (downward).

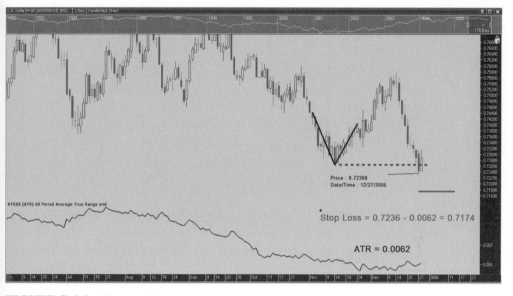

FIGURE 3.11 The stop loss
Source: Reproduced by permission of *Market Analyst.*

The seventh rule is to define the opposite swing between our new low and the previous low. In our example, the opposite swing is a "mountain peak." This peak will be the target for our profitable exit, as illustrated in Figure 3.12.

The die is cast, and we enter this trade with both expectation and acceptance. Based on our understanding of this pattern, we can expect a 70 percent probability of success. This also means that we can also expect a 30 percent probability of this trade ending up as a loss. We have to accept either result, and the planning of this trade tells that we will exit, and accept our loss at the stop loss level. Our trade plan also calls upon us to accept our profit at the exit target. This exit target is at 0.7578. We accept our profit at this exit target because our understanding of the sideways market suggests that buying forces are more likely to weaken at the resistance ceiling, and as *aiki* traders, we want to act in harmony with how markets behave.

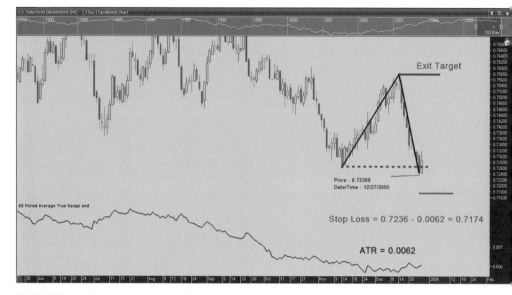

FIGURE 3.12 Mountain peak target
Source: Reproduced by permission of *Market Analyst.*

It is essential that we stress the utility and importance of a trade plan, especially for the serious trader. Firstly, any good trade plan is based on a robust and fundamental principle that has been proven to achieve a statistically positive result. In this case, we begin with the expanded sideways range principle, and we will specifically hunt for this particular pattern and trade it when the market action matches our trade rules.

Secondly, the trade plan allows us to manage the uncertainty of the market and the emotions that such uncertainty will engender in us after we enter the trade.

Thirdly, the trade plan will allow us to visualize what the market has to look like if we are likely to be wrong (triggering the stop loss) or what the market is likely to look like if we are correct (moving toward the profit exit target).

Once the trade is triggered, we just have to patiently wait for the market to trigger the stop loss or the exit target, and accept either result calmly, as in Figure 3.13.

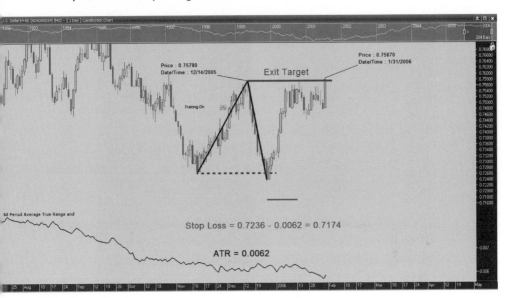

FIGURE 3.13 The trade plan
Source: Reproduced by permission of *Market Analyst.*

Let us recap the rules that will define and trade the expanded sideways range pattern:

1. Define the floor and the ceiling.
2. Wait for the market to trade above the ceiling, or to trade below the floor.
3. Entry rule:
   a. Sell at the close if the market closes below the prior ceiling.
   b. Buy at the close if the market closes above the prior floor.
4. Stop loss exit rule:
   a. Insert the 60-period ATR tool (ATR60).
   b. Use ATR60 as a filter:
      i. If the market triggers a sell trade, the formula is:
      Stop Loss = New High + ATR60
      ii. If the market triggers a buy trade, the formula is:
      Stop Loss = New Low − ATR60

5. Profit taking exit rule:

    a. Exit target is the opposite extreme between your defined entry and the prior swing:

        i. If the market triggers a buy trade, then the exit must be the mountain high between your entry and the prior valley swing low.

        ii. If the market triggers a sell trade, then the exit is the valley low between your entry and the previous mountain swing high.

Look at Figures 3.14, 3.15, 3.16, and 3.17. It will be important for us to practice with past historical charts and learn how to spot this particular pattern. It is similar to a beginner martial artist practicing and refining one single technique that resolves a single particular situation. Repeated practice will lead to conscious competence, and eventually to an instinctive ability to recognize and act whenever this particular situation presents itself.

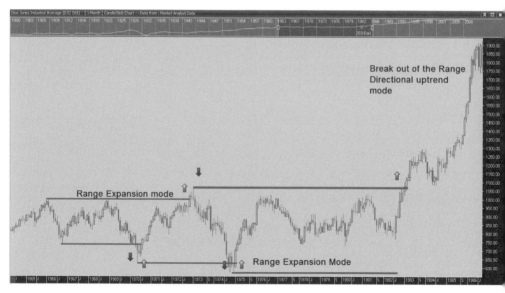

FIGURE 3.14 Expanded sideways pattern
Source: Reproduced by permission of *Market Analyst.*

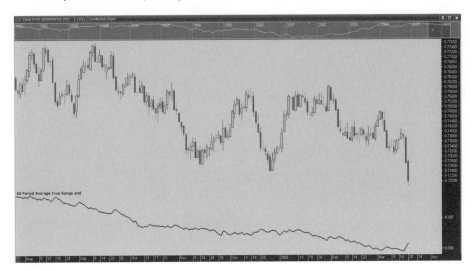

FIGURE 3.15 Ex 1. Spot the expanded sideways pattern
Source: Reproduced by permission of *Market Analyst.*

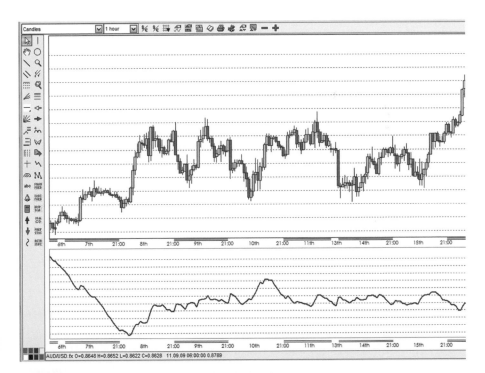

FIGURE 3.16 Ex 2. Spot the expanded sideways pattern
Source: GFT's DealBook® 360 Trading.

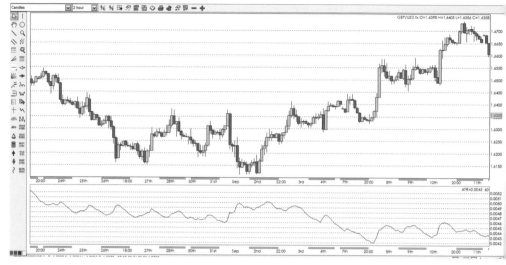

FIGURE 3.17 Ex 3. Spot the expanded sideways pattern
Source: GFT's DealBook® 360 Trading.

QUALIFYING THE TRADE

We have just started to understand how markets can behave when in a sideways range pattern. We now need to enhance our understanding so that we can elect either to trade the signal, or ignore the trade.

The key consideration in accepting the inherent risk of any trade is to correctly assess whether the reward justifies the risk that will have to be assumed. The martial analogy is to compare the trader to a commanding general. Like the trader, the general has finite resources that have to be conserved. It will make sense to commit his forces to battle if he has a higher chance of success. In addition, the rewards and pleasure of victory must significantly outweigh the costs and pain of defeat.

Let us now review our trade plan. We are able to define an entry, a stop loss exit, and also a profit exit. Let us look at Figure 3.18.

The entry bar is the close of the bullish candle (0.7286). We can then determine the expected loss, which is simply the difference

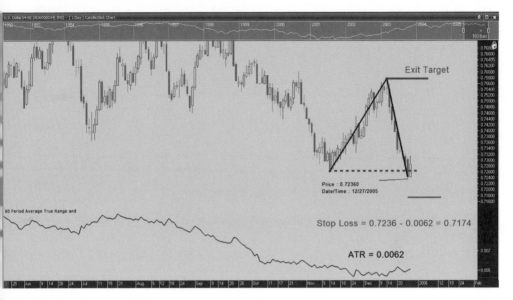

FIGURE 3.18 Expanded sideways buy trade
Source: Reproduced by permission of *Market Analyst.*

between the entry price and the stop loss price. As our entry was at 0.7286, and the stop loss level was calculated to be 0.7174, our expected loss is 0.0112.

The next step is to determine the expected profit, which is the difference between the exit price and the entry price (Figures 3.19 and 3.20).

The exit target is 0.7578, and as our entry level is at 0.7286, we can easily calculate our expected profit to be 0.0292. We can then calculate the reward to risk ratio by dividing the expected profit by the expected loss. In this example, as the expected profit is 0.0292, and the expected loss is 0.0112, the reward to risk ratio is 2.61.

This means that for an expected loss of 1 unit, we can expect a potential profit of 2.61 units. Obviously, it will benefit us to accept and execute trades that have a superior reward to risk ratio. So what constitutes a superior reward to risk ratio? What number do we want to use in order to qualify a "go" or a "no go" for the trade that we are analyzing? Can an optimum reward to risk ratio be defined?

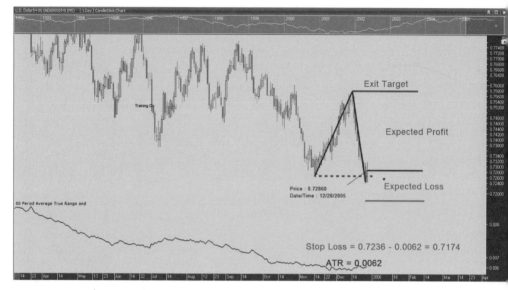

FIGURE 3.19 Reward and risk
Source: Reproduced by permission of *Market Analyst.*

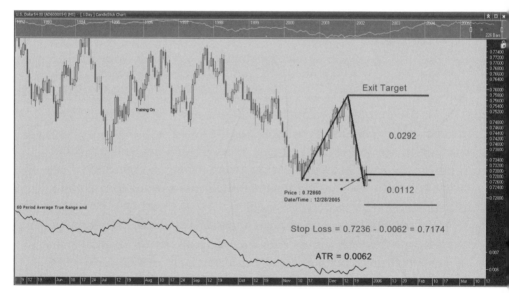

FIGURE 3.20 Determine reward and risk
Source: Reproduced by permission of *Market Analyst.*

We can answer this crucial question by considering the statistics of the turtle traders.

We know that over time, the turtles have a hit rate of 30 percent, the hit rate being defined as the percentage of profitable trade. Therefore their miss rate (or loss trades) will account for 70 percent of total trades. We also need to define the average dollar win and the average dollar loss. This is simply the average return from each winning trade and the average cost of each losing trade, and is usually expressed in the trader's base or home currency.

Let us now calculate the reward to risk ratio that will mathematically result in a zero gain, zero loss scenario. This will imply that total loss will be equal to total profits:

$$\text{Total Profit} = \text{Total Loss}$$

$$\text{Total Profit} = (\text{Hit Rate} \times \text{Average \$ Win})$$

$$\text{Total Loss} = (\text{Miss Rate} \times \text{Average \$ Loss}).$$

Therefore, in order to calculate the border or cut-off number where there is a zero gain and zero loss, we can state this equation as:

$$(\text{Hit Rate} \times \text{Average \$ Win}) = (\text{Miss Rate} \times \text{Average \$ Loss});$$

$$\text{Therefore } (\text{Average \$ Win}/\text{Average \$ Loss}) = (\text{Miss Rate}/\text{Hit Rate});$$

We know the turtle hit rate is 30 percent and the miss rate is 70 percent.

The "Average $ Win" to "Average $ Loss" ratio can also be simplified as the reward to risk ratio, expressed as the units of reward for one unit of risk, and in this example what we are calculating is the reward to risk ratio that will lead to a break-even situation. Again, in this example, the turtles will break even if the ratio of their average dollar win to average dollar loss is 2.33.

Let me restate that the reward to risk ratio will define the units of profit for one unit of loss. In our example in Figure 3.18 the reward to risk ratio is 2.61, which means that we will have a reward of 2.61 units for a potential loss of 1 unit.

Now this is a trade that captures the expanded sideways range, where the hit rate is expected to be 70 percent and the miss rate is expected to be 30 percent. Therefore, using the same formula and substituting the correct numbers into the equation, we can calculate the break-even reward risk ratio for the expanded sideways range pattern. This works out to be 0.42.

What this number suggests is that given the statistics of the expanded sideways range pattern, we can accept a statistical minimum reward to risk ratio of 0.42 and still emerge without damage, albeit without gain either. Obviously, we will want to engage in overall profitable trading, so it will be in our interest to have the reward to risk ratio as high as is practically possible.

We must also understand the nature of probability, and its impact on real life trading. Have you ever been shown a unit trust or mutual fund sales brochure? Invariably, the performance chart starts off with a gain, and then shows some minor dip, and thereafter, performance results continue to show trending characteristics. Real-life experience can show that our initial investment may start off with a loss instead of the advertised profit. What this means is that the distribution of results (either profit or loss) can be random, but over time, the long-term statistics will prevail. This is a critical point that must be understood and internalized if we are to succeed in trading.

This brings us back to the break-even reward to risk ratio. If we choose to trade with near break-even reward to risk ratio, we will have many more trades, but we will not be able to sustain a series of losses initially, especially if the losses do actually occur in the initial stages of our trading career. On the other hand, if we select a very high reward to risk ratio as the entry qualification, then we are likely to engage in very few trades. The ideal is probably somewhere in between either extreme.

I personally trigger a trade only if the reward to risk ratio is above 1.80. However, you may elect to trade with a reward to risk ratio of 1.30 so that you can experience more trades initially. There is a caveat here; in this phase of our training, we will have to trade in very small sizes. My personal experience will illustrate why this is important. When I was first introduced to the game of *mahjong*, I was learning to play with bet sizes that resulted in an average profit or loss of $800 per session. My circle of friends engaged in twice-weekly sessions. I soon realized that I was learning the game very expensively, precisely because beginners like me are bound to make mistakes and such mistakes are usually loss-making mistakes! On hindsight, I should have started my learning sessions with average stakes of $80 per session.

Similarly in trading, we can choose the bet size of our learning experience. What I can suggest is that we initially trade in very small trade sizes in order to minimize the cost of learning. Make all the mistakes we need to make, and learn from our mistakes, but ensure that these mistakes are not financially fatal. Once we have completed at least 30 trades, we will have some experience and some statistics about our own trading. When we gain more experience, our competency will also improve. It is only at this stage that we can begin to trade with bigger stakes.

We will end Chapter 3 with a finalized version of the rules to trade the expanded sideways range pattern:

1. Define the floor and the ceiling.
2. Wait for the market to trade above the ceiling, or to trade below the floor.
3. Entry rule:

    a. Sell at the close if the market closes below the prior ceiling;

    b. Buy at the close if the market closes above the prior floor.
4. Stop loss exit rule:

    a. Insert the 60ATR tool;

    b. Use the ATR as a filter:

    i. If the market triggers a sell trade, the formula is:
    $$\text{Stop Loss} = \text{New High} + \text{ATR}$$

    ii. If the market triggers a buy trade, the formula is:
    $$\text{Stop Loss} = \text{New Low} - \text{ATR}$$

5. Profit-taking exit rule:

   a. Exit target is the opposite extreme between your defined entry and the prior swing:

      i. If the market triggers a buy trade, then the exit must be the mountain high between your entry and the valley swing low.

      ii. If the market triggers a sell trade, then the exit is the valley low between your entry and the previous mountain swing high.

6. Trade qualification rule:

   a. Execute a trade if the reward to risk ratio is larger than 1.3;

   b. Avoid a trade if the reward to risk ratio is lower than 1.3.

At this point, it will be good to touch on the mindset that we should develop in order to succeed as a profitable trader. There will be traders who appear to be spectacularly successful over short periods, but many eventually lose and fail over the long term. The successful trader is not only profitable, but is profitable over time. How do they achieve this?

I believe that any successful trader acts only when he understands the behavior of the market. If he does not understand the market, he will not trade in it. This is similar to the *samurai* in combat. The successful combatant is looking for his opponent to be off balance. Once this occurs, he is able to execute his technique that suits this particular opening that he recognizes and understands. His training is to recognize this off-balance point, and then act decisively. If he cannot perceive this moment of off balance, he will not commit to his technique and his attack.

We have just ended this chapter that is devoted to the expanded sideways range pattern. I strongly suggest that we trade this pattern when we see and recognize it. If the market is not in this particular pattern, then we will choose to avoid combat because our current knowledge does not yet allow us to understand and assess our probability of success. Our initial function is to gain competency and then master this very first pattern.

Remember, trade only what we can understand, and avoid what we do not understand. Both practice and experience will sharpen our understanding and our execution. There is no shortcut to this learning process. We will have to put in the time, effort, energy, and commitment in order to achieve success—in trading, in the martial arts, and in life in general.

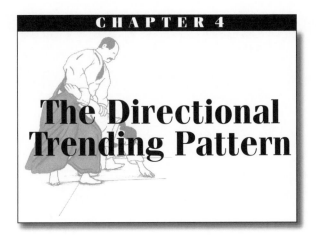

CHAPTER 4

The Directional Trending Pattern

I started off the early part of this book with a description of how markets go through periods of expansion and periods of contraction. The swing lines in Figure 4.1 illustrate the expansion and contraction that is evident when the market is in a directional trend.

The contraction mode itself can assume different formats. In Chapter 3, we looked at one specific format that the contraction mode can take. This is the expanded sideways range pattern.

Please observe Figures 4.1 and 4.2. What is the most distinguishing difference between the expansion (impulse) and the contraction (correction) mode?

The key distinguishing feature of the impulse is that it is significantly larger than the correction. The turtle traders have also noticed this particular characteristic, and their trading method and philosophy is to hunt for the large impulse and its attendant large profit. They do this by recognizing the correction phase, but they do not trade the correction because the correction mode is relatively small in size. Turtle traders trade once they believe the correction phase is over, and

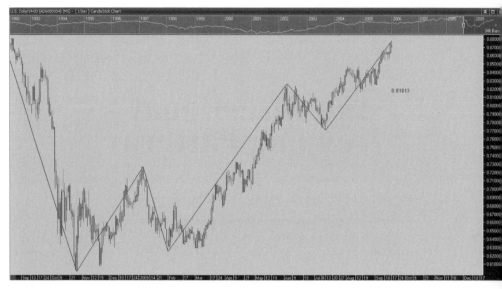

FIGURE 4.1 Expansion and contraction
Source: Reproduced by permission of *Market Analyst*.

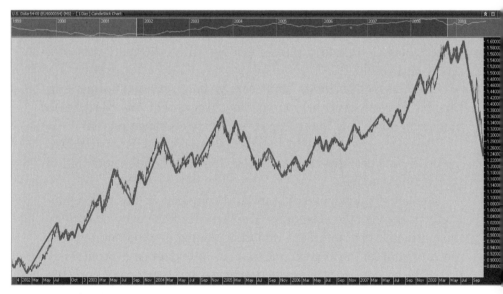

FIGURE 4.2 Impulse and correction
Source: Reproduced by permission of *Market Analyst*.

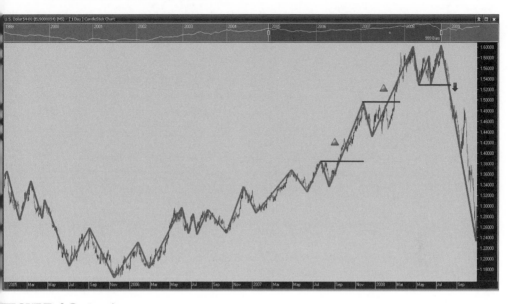

FIGURE 4.3 Breakout
Source: Reproduced by permission of *Market Analyst.*

their specific entry method is to trade on the breakout of the correction phase (Figure 4.3).

In this chapter, we will expand our knowledge to include the basic impulse correction impulse pattern. For the purpose of this book, we will call this pattern the type 1 trend pattern. Again, let me state that the type 1 trend pattern is just one version of how markets can behave in a trend. Again, our philosophy for now is to only understand the type 1 trend pattern, and trade it when it occurs; remember, we will ignore situations we do not comprehend. In its most basic format, the correction mode separates two impulses. Also, we make the following assumptions that the correction is simple and the impulse that follows this simple correction is at least as large as, or larger than the impulse that comes before the correction.

We will use the moving average as the tool that will define the impulse and the correction phase of a directional market. The moving average also serves to define the timeframe of the trend we intend to analyze and trade. The moving average also serves to smooth out the candle-by-candle gyrations that can sometimes confuse us (see Figure 4.4).

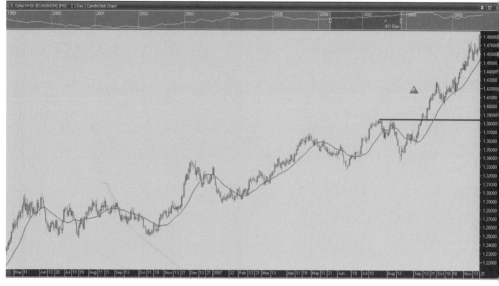

FIGURE 4.4   Moving average superimposed
Source: Reproduced by permission of *Market Analyst.*

Figure 4.4 illustrates the type 1 trend pattern. This is a candle-stick chart with a moving average that is superimposed on the chart. Notice that the moving average smooths out the candle-to-candle fluctuations. Figure 4.5 shows the same moving average without the candles.

Notice that the moving average itself can display sideways range characteristics, as well as the impulse, correction, and impulse pattern.

This chapter focuses on the type 1 trend pattern so Figure 4.6 will label the impulse, the correction, and the next impulse that is the essential nature of the type 1 trend pattern. It is important to note that the type 1 trend pattern can, but may not necessarily repeat itself.

Let us now turn to Figure 4.7. We want to formulate a consistent way to identify the impulse and the correction using both the candles as well as the moving average. We can see that this market has generally higher highs and higher lows and so we recognize a bullish trending market. Notice that the impulses will be pointing up. Here are the rules you will use to identify the up impulse:

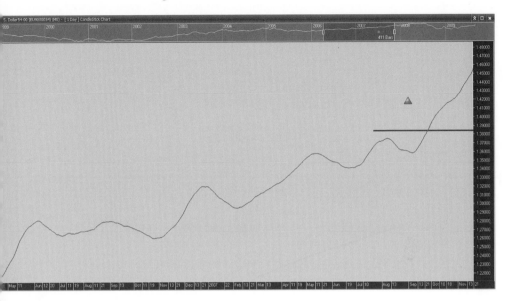

FIGURE 4.5 Moving average only
Source: Reproduced by permission of *Market Analyst.*

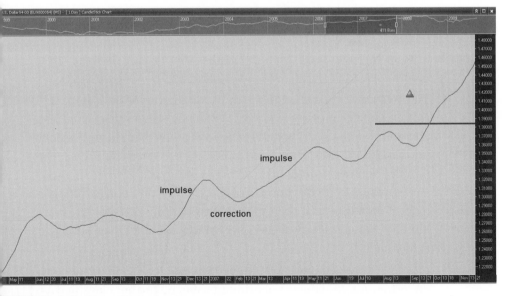

FIGURE 4.6 Type 1 trend pattern
Source: Reproduced by permission of *Market Analyst.*

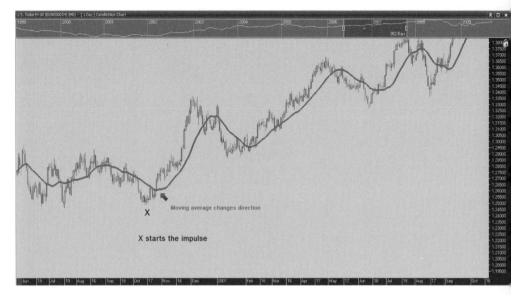

FIGURE 4.7 Identify impulse
Source: Reproduced by permission of *Market Analyst.*

1. The moving average must change direction from down to up.
2. The impulse starts from the low before the moving average changes direction. We label this low as "X" in our chart.
3. The up impulse must then cut above the moving average till it reaches its high point, which we label as "A" (Figure 4.8).
4. The market then turns down in a correction, as in Figure 4.9. Notice that the moving average itself also changes direction. The correction ends at B, which is the low point that starts the next impulse. Also note that from point A, the correction cuts the moving average to reach B.

    Obviously, if we know for sure that the correction has indeed ended, it will then make sense to buy at B for the next impulse move to C. However, in real life, we are never sure that B has ended.
5. In the art of trading, we know that we can only deal with uncertainties, and these uncertainties can be further classified as:

    a. Good quality low-risk high-reward opportunities;

    b. Poor quality highly uncertain and risky opportunities; and

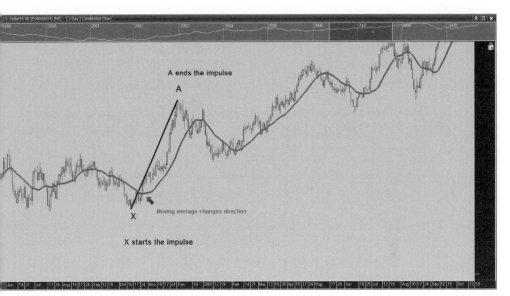

FIGURE 4.8 Impulse identification
Source: Reproduced by permission of *Market Analyst.*

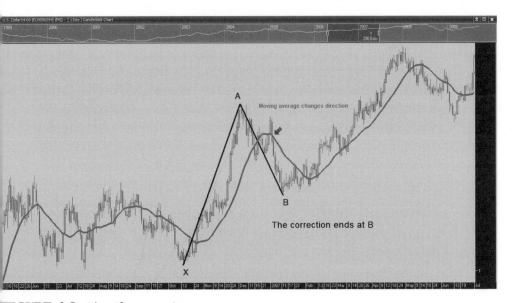

FIGURE 4.9 Identify correction
Source: Reproduced by permission of *Market Analyst.*

c. We only want to execute trades that we assess as belonging to category a, and not those in category b.

6. We will assume that the correction B low is most probable only when the market closes above the moving average (Figure 4.10).

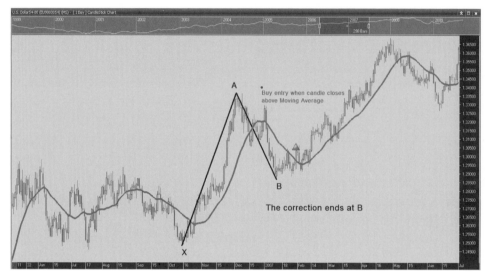

FIGURE 4.10 Correction ends
Source: Reproduced by permission of *Market Analyst.*

7. The impulse then resumes and ends at C Figure 4.11).

8. In *aiki* trading terms, we have waited for the market to display in this case, buying strength in XA, and we have patiently waited for the corrective AB. We assess that the AB selling correction is weak, and we will enter as a buyer, in direct opposition to the AB seller. The *aikido* imagery in our minds is to enter directly once the strong buyer displays his strength and intention (see illustrations on page 65).

We can use a similar set of rules to define the bearish impulse, the weak buying rally and the bearish continuation impulse (Figure 4.12):

1. The moving average must change direction from up to down.

2. The impulse starts from the high before the moving average turns down. We label this high as "X" in our chart.

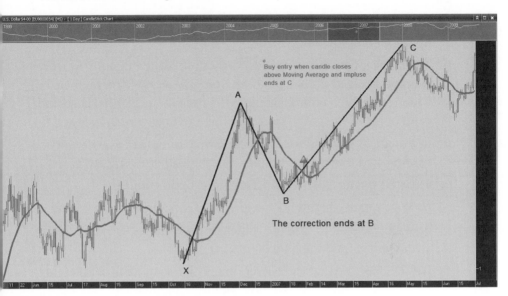

FIGURE 4.11 Bullish type 1 trend pattern
Source: Reproduced by permission of *Market Analyst.*

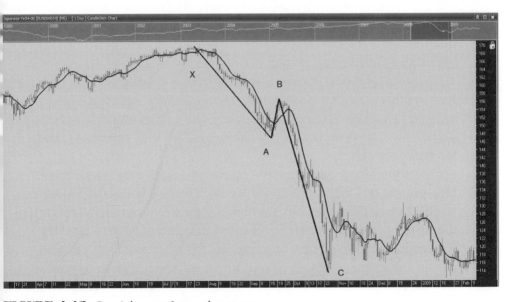

FIGURE 4.12 Bearish type 1 trend pattern
Source: Reproduced by permission of *Market Analyst.*

3. The down impulse must then cut below the moving average until it reaches its low at "A."

4. The market then turns up in a correction. Notice that the moving average itself also changes direction. The correction ends at B, which is the high point that starts the next impulse. Also note that from point A, the correction cuts the moving average to reach B.

5. In the art of trading, we know that we can only deal with uncertainties, and these uncertainties can be further classified as:

   a. Good quality low-risk high-reward opportunities;

   b. Poor quality highly uncertain and risky opportunities, and

   c. We only want to execute trades that we assess as belonging to category a, and not those in category b.

6. We will assume that the correction B high is most probable only when the market closes below the moving average.

What we now need to note is that the moving average defines the timeframe, the impulse, the correction and also the entry signal for the start of the next continuation impulse.

The setup process for the type 1 trend pattern trade is to first wait for the formation of the XAB pattern. We then assume that the market can then trade the impulse continuation, which is how we have defined as the completion of the type 1 trend pattern. The trade is triggered by a market close either above the moving average for a bullish buy entry, or a close below the moving average for a bearish sell entry (refer back to Figures 4.11 and 4.12). Remember the *aikido* metaphor: If we can detect a weak buyer, we will enter once the strong seller emerges.

I wish to stress again that the market does not care whether we have bought or sold; the market will go wherever it will go regardless of our trading positions, our emotional hopes, and our fears. Therefore every trade that we take will result in either a win or a loss. We have to accept not only the pleasure and joy of the winners, but also accept the discomfort and pain of any loss. Again, I wish to stress that the path to success is to ensure that our loss is controlled and is within both our financial as well as our psychological tolerance.

IDENTIFYING AND TRADING A TYPE 1 TREND PATTERN

In our trading plan for the type 1 trend pattern, we have identified step 6 as the assumption that the continuation impulse is likely to occur. We then enter a trade in the direction of the expected impulse to C. We will now practice with a historical example of how this pattern can be identified and traded.

Ask whether the current market on the right-hand side of the chart is more likely sideways or more likely impulse in the timeframe you select. For this exercise, we will use a 21-period simple moving average, basis close as the tool to define both timeframe as well as trend. This moving average will be now referred to as MA21. Firstly ask: What is the direction of MA21? If we identify that the market is in impulse, we then label X as the start of the impulse. Look at Figure 4.13, and attempt to answer the questions above. We should be able to see that MA21 is pointing down. In

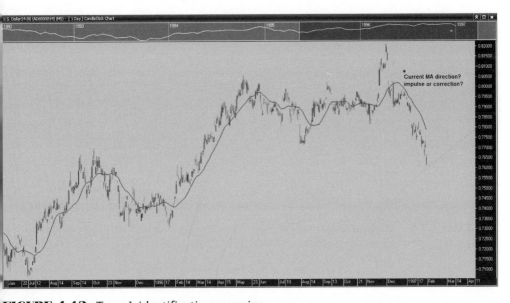

FIGURE 4.13 Type 1 identification exercise
Source: Reproduced by permission of *Market Analyst*.

addition, MA21 is currently below the previous MA21 low, and this suggests that the market is either sideways, or could be in the early stages of the type 1 trend pattern. In addition, the size of the current move does not appear to be a small corrective move, but seems more likely to be an impulse.

Figure 4.14 illustrates this labeling process. The bearish downward impulse starts at X, but why do we label A with a question mark? We do so because the market has not confirmed the impulse low, and if the market impulse continues downward, then A will be located and labeled differently. We will only assume that the impulse ends at A when the moving average itself shows a change of direction. In Figure 4.14, the moving average is still pointing downward, so we assume that there has been no correction in this timeframe defined by the 21-period moving average.

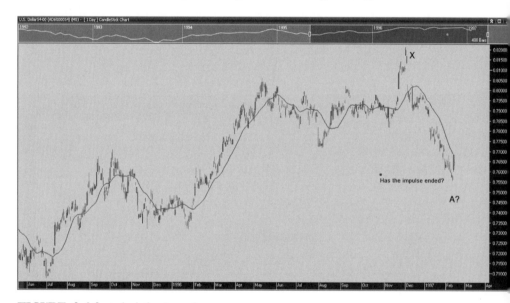

FIGURE 4.14 Label the impulse
Source: Reproduced by permission of *Market Analyst.*

In Figure 4.15, the market stages a correction. This correction is defined by MA21 changing its direction of movement, in this case from down to up.

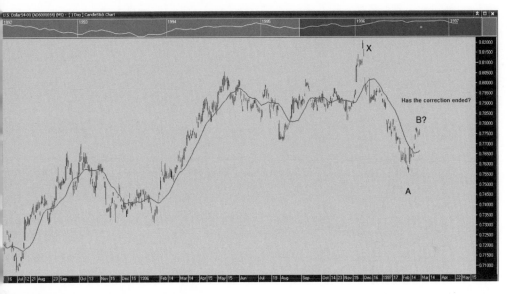

FIGURE 4.15 Label the correction
Source: Reproduced by permission of *Market Analyst.*

We now assume that the impulse has ended at A and remove the question mark. To recap, we have identified the impulse XA. Again we now place a question mark with B, precisely because we are questioning when this correction can end or has ended. As long as the market in this example closes above the moving average, we assume that B? is still work in progress.

In Figure 4.16, we now observe that the market has traded and closed below MA21. We now assume that the correction has ended, and we will now remove the question mark from B. Our identification process has now labeled the impulse as XA, and also the correction as AB.

The close below MA21 not only assumes the end of the correction at B, but also assumes that the market is now in the early stages of the continuation of the next impulse. In other words, after the weak buyer in the correction is unable to continue, the strong seller reasserts control of the market. Let us revisit the illustrations in Chapter 1 to reiterate this from a martial arts perspective.

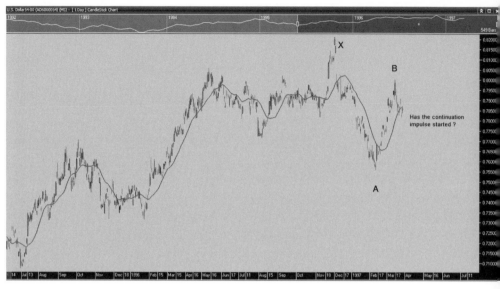

FIGURE 4.16 Correction ends
Source: Reproduced by permission of *Market Analyst.*

Therefore, the close below MA21 acts as the trade and action trigger. Remember, the type 1 trend pattern has two impulses separated by a correction; both impulses are in the same direction, and the direction of the correction is always opposite to the direction of the impulses. Therefore, in this case we are now expecting a downward impulse move approximately equal to the size of the initial XA downward impulse, and we have initiated a sell trade because we are trading our belief in how the type 1 trend pattern should behave. In our minds, this belief also incorporates the *aikido* principle of attacking directly when the opponent is weak.

To restate again, the martial arts philosophy is to attack when your enemy is weak. In this case, as the buy force is assumed to be a weak correction, our stance will be to sell once the buy force peters out. We can then expect to join the direction of a new selling impulse, and therefore be in phase and harmony with the prevailing trend.

Controlling the weak force
Illustration by Deepak Ram Ayengar and Yong Jie Yu.

Once we have initiated a trade, we can only control how we exit our trade. It is critically important to remember that we can never control the direction of any market, and that the market will move without considering our trade, our intentions and our emotions. If the market agrees with our analysis of its probable behavior, then we will be rewarded with a profit. If the market disagrees with our analysis, we will suffer a loss.

We now need to be able to determine what the market will look like if our analysis is wrong. This will allow us to plan an exit strategy when the market moves contrary to our preferred profitable and pleasurable scenario.

PLANNING THE STOP LOSS EXIT

In planning and executing this trade, we have assumed that the correction has ended at B. Therefore if the market moves above B (after we have entered a sell trade), then we have to recognize that the correction phase is still a work in progress, and that the expected impulse is not yet ready to occur as we expect.

The problem lies in defining the "breathing space" that we wish to allow for an adverse move against us. Most traders will typically say that any move above B invalidates the type 1 trend pattern. Unfortunately, the market has a tendency to frustrate as many market participants as much of the time as possible, so it is best to devise a "stealthy" exit strategy that is not used by the majority of traders.

The generic tool that we can apply is the 60-period Average True Range. This is a tool that calculates the average movement of the past 60 candles. We will now apply this average movement as a filter to B. If the market moves above B by the value of ATR60, then we recognize that the market correction is probably still ongoing, and that B is still probably not complete. Figure 4.17 shows the ATR tool and the entry trigger. Figure 4.18 shows the calculation and insertion of the stop loss level.

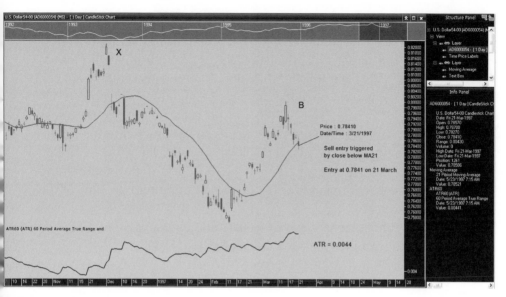

FIGURE 4.17 ATR tool and trade entry trigger
Source: Reproduced by permission of *Market Analyst.*

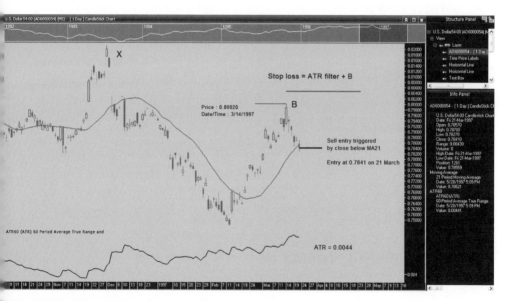

FIGURE 4.18 The stop loss
Source: Reproduced by permission of *Market Analyst.*

The initiating sell entry was at 0.7841, when the market closed below MA21. One common objection is that the trader may not know whether the market will or will not trigger the trade upon the close of business. This is an invalid objection. The onus is on the trader to monitor the market once the impulse XA and the correction (B?) is tentatively formed. The ATR60 can be used as a guide to assess whether very detailed attention needs to be directed to the potential trade setup. If the market's close is within the value of ATR60 from the trade's trigger, then it is the duty of the serious and dedicated trader to monitor the market at or around the time of the market's close.

The B high has a value of 0.8002, and as the value of ATR60 is 0.0044, the stop loss level is calculated as 0.8046.

THE STRUCTURAL RISK

We have learned to identify a type 1 trend pattern, and we have also learned how to set a "stealthy" stop loss. I use the term "stealthy" to mean that the stop loss exit level is set sufficiently far away to allow for adverse price movement. The stop loss level will also acknowledge that a penetration of the said stop loss level will suggest that our trade assumptions are probably incorrect. What this means is that we will exit a trade that is probably incorrect.

We can therefore define the structural loss risk of every trade as the difference between the structurally defined entry level and the stealthy stop loss level. The value of this difference is the trade's expected loss (Figure 4.19). Our entry is at 0.7841 on March 21, and as our stop loss is at 0.8046, the expected loss is therefore 0.0205.

The Profit Exit Strategy

We have calculated the structural risk inherent in the trade. This accounts for the loss-making scenario. We must also plan our action to exit with a profit should the market behave as we anticipate.

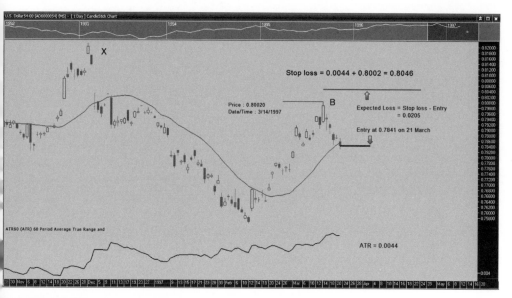

FIGURE 4.19 Expected trade loss
Source: Reproduced by permission of *Market Analyst.*

Again, we default to the reward to risk ratio, and at this stage we will be happy with a reward to risk ratio of at least 1.80. In Figure 4.19, we have a structural risk of 0.0205 pips, so we can now calculate that we will exit this trade by placing a profit taking buy order to lock in at the minimum, an expected profit of 0.0369 pips (0.0205 × 1.80). As we initiated a sell trade at 0.7841, this will mean that our profit-taking level has to be set at 0.7472 (entry-expected profit).

Again, let me reiterate the benefit of a trade plan; it will help us handle the uncertainty and the emotional stress that will afflict all traders once we have an open position. With this trade plan, we know where we will exit this trade, and whether the trade results in a profit or a loss, we will accept either result with calmness. We then proceed to wait for either the loss or the profit to be realized (Figures 4.20 and 4.21).

Can the new impulse continue? The short answer is yes. The impulse can continue. So why did we exit? We exited because

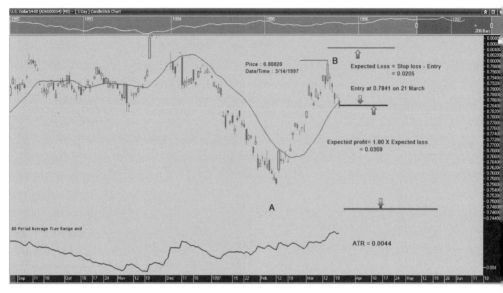

FIGURE 4.20 The stop loss exit and the profit exit plan
Source: Reproduced by permission of *Market Analyst.*

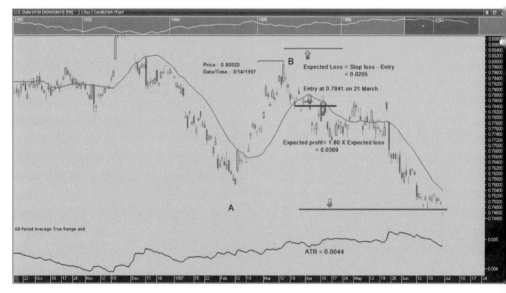

FIGURE 4.21 The market decides the trade result
Source: Reproduced by permission of *Market Analyst.*

at this stage of our learning process, we are trying to build up an "experience bank." This will allow us to have more opportunities to practice the recognition of the type 1 trend pattern. The more experience we gain, the more competent we will become in planning the trade and in implementing the entry and the exit strategies.

We will continue searching our trading universe for this pattern and we intend to execute at least 30 such examples of the type 1 trend pattern. We can then analyze each trade to check whether our execution of the plan was well done or not. Assuming competent trade execution, the trade results will determine whether a type 1 trend pattern can generate a positive result. As we intend to do at least 30 such trades, the results of this experiment will hold some statistical validity, as the results are based not on a few results but over at least 30 results for the type 1 trend pattern.

TIMEFRAME, AND THE SELECTION OF ITS RELEVANT MOVING AVERAGE VALUE

In the example that we used, the moving average that was selected was the 21-period simple moving average based on the close. We have a choice of Fibonacci numbers that we can select, but the number that we use has to reflect a logical period.

Fibonacci is the name by which we identify a famous 13th century mathematician. His name was Leonardo, *filius* Bonacci, which means Leonardo, son of Bonacci. Over the centuries, *filius* Bonacci eventually became Fibonacci. We will be studying how Fibonacci theory is applied to trading, and a more detailed explanation will be found in Chapter 7, but as we intend to use some Fibonacci numbers in this chapter, a quick explanation is now offered.

Fibonacci discovered a mathematical formula that starts with just two integer numbers, namely 0 and 1. The next number in the

Fibonacci sequence will be the sum of the previous two numbers. Therefore, the Fibonacci sequence will appear as:

0, 1, 1, 2, 3, 5, 8, 13, 21, 34, 55, 89, 144, 233 . . . . . .

In this chapter, we will be using Fibonacci numbers 8, 21, 55, and 233.

There are five trading days in a week, so a simple moving average 5 will represent the trend of the weekly timeframe. We can choose to replace MA5 with MA8. If we select MA8 as the moving average that best reflects the weekly timeframe, then we will consistently continue to use MA8 for all our analysis.

Using the same logic, there are approximately 22 trading days in a calendar month, so if we select the 21-period MA on the daily chart, the movements of MA21 will represent the trend of the monthly timeframe. Let me clarify: The trend does not last for just one month. However, the sideways patterns that MA21 can create and the correction impulse patterns that MA21 can also create will show the trend of MA21 and therefore show the trend of the monthly time frame.

There are approximately 65 working days in the quarter of the year, so MA55 will best represent the trend of the quarterly timeframe.

Similarly, there are about 260 working days in a year, so MA233 will best reflect the yearly timeframe.

Therefore, the Fibonacci numbers that we will use in our moving average method are 8, 21, 55 and 233. This set of numbers can be applied to either the end of day chart (the daily chart), or on any intraday timeframe, an example of which can be the end of hour chart (the hourly chart).

Figure 4.22 displays both MA8, and MA21. We can make one very important observation. The line direction of MA21 determines the trend of MA8. We have labeled the MA21 impulse as XA. Within XA, the shorter time frame MA8 traded the type 1 trend pattern. It is self evident and also intuitively obvious that the size of the movements in the lower timeframe is generally smaller than the size of the movements in the higher timeframe.

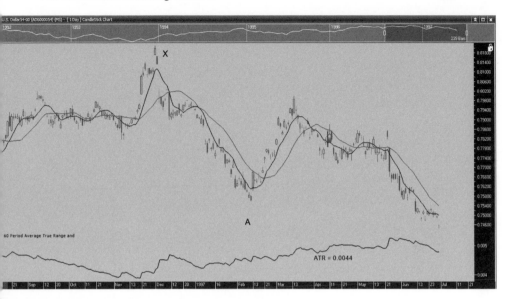

FIGURE 4.22 Displaying both MA8 and MA21
Source: Reproduced by permission of *Market Analyst.*

This is a very important observation and also a very important aspect of market understanding. We can compare this to the idea of circular motion in martial arts. Within a big circle, there are also different applications of smaller circles. The big circle may be obvious to the beginner, but the smaller circle may be beyond the beginner's perception.

A beginner's understanding and development will progress once he can learn to see the complexities of the small circles within the larger circle. Similarly, the *aiki* trader must progress and develop. He must be able to see, visualize, and understand the nature of the larger timeframe's impact (the big circle) on the lower timeframe's trend (the smaller set of circles).

Figure 4.23 displays MA55 and MA233. Note that we will use the exponential calculation to derive the values of MA55 and MA233, while MA8 and MA21 will use the simple calculation method.

Can we also see the characteristic behavior and the relationship between the timeframes? When MA233 is swinging downward, MA55

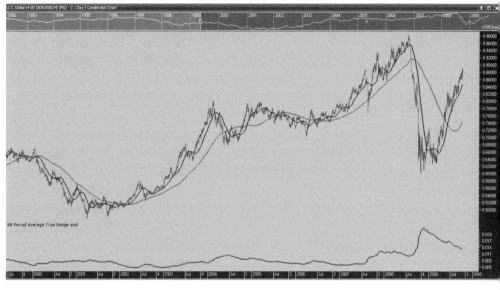

FIGURE 4.23 MA55 and MA 233
Source: Reproduced by permission of *Market Analyst.*

is and most likely will be in a downtrend; when MA233 is pointing upward, MA55 is and most likely will be in an uptrend. Can we also observe that the type 1 trend pattern can be defined by using MA55 as the trading timeframe? This observation leads us to conclude that market behavior is fractal in nature, with the direction of the higher timeframe clearly indicating the probable trend of the lower time-frame. This principle is robust, and can be applied to any freely traded financial instrument, be it FX, equities or futures.

If we eventually decide to trade intraday candles, we can then employ the same moving averages (MA8, MA21, MA55, and MA233) to define the timeframe and its related trend on the intraday chart. Note that we will use the simple moving average calculation for MA8 and MA21, and the exponential moving average calculation for MA55 and MA233. We will have confidence in the robustness of our method because it is based on the fractal nature of market behavior. So far, we have studied two aspects of market behavior. The type 1 trend pattern, and the expanded sideways range pattern can occur in any timeframe, and we can elect to trade the timeframe that best suits our psyche and personality. It will now be appropriate to discuss the matching of the time frame to the trader's personality.

A somewhat "hyperactive" trader has a behavior pattern that requires constant, perhaps even frantic activity. This requirement for constant activity in trading will translate to a requirement to use a shorter-term timeframe. The more hyperactive we are, the shorter will be our preferred timeframe. An example of a very short-term timeframe is where each single candlestick can represent a time period of, say, 15 minutes. The analogy with martial arts is to compare the hyperactive trader to a very close-range combatant who can engage in a flurry of quick exchanges of attack, defense, and counterattack.

A patient trader will be more inclined to trade for a wider profit margin. Typically, the patient trader will be looking to trade the trend of the monthly, and MA21 is probably his definition of trend. Lower time frame trends, say, in the hourly timeframe, may be "noise" to the patient trader. The patient trader may of course use lower timeframe signals to enter the market if he chooses to be aggressive when he is in a low-risk zone as defined by his timeframe. The martial analogy here is to compare the patient trader to the long-range combatant, who is looking for a major campaign, instead of a series of minor engagements. Nonetheless, once he detects that his low-risk high-probability opportunity to strike is at hand, he may decide to aggressively engage with a close combat method, in order to gain an early advantage should he be correct in his assessment of the situation. Obviously, the resources and capital that will be required for a patient positional trader will be very different from the capital that is required of the short-term hyperactive trader. The timeframe that we will choose will therefore be defined by our self-understanding and also the financial muscle at hand. Remember the advice of Sun Tzu: The successful trader must not only know the market, but must also know himself. Only then will we be able to match the appropriate timeframe to our own personality.

We will next look at the successful breakout pattern in order to widen our understanding. With new knowledge and understanding, new trading opportunities can be recognized and exploited.

CHAPTER 5

The Successful Breakout

O ur journey started with the study of the expanded sideways range pattern. The trading premise of the expanded side-ways range pattern is that 70 percent of breakout attempts fail to impulse, and instead revert to the sideways range. Therefore, there is a 30 percent probability that any breakout of an expanded sideways range pattern can succeed. This chapter is our attempt to define the factors and conditions that suggest a successful breakout from the sideways range.

Our journey then continued with the examination of the type 1 trend pattern. There are two fundamental principles or require-ments that define the type 1 trend pattern. The first is that there must be an impulse move, which is part of a directional trend. The second requirement is that there is some form of correction or slowdown. After the correction ends, the market is then poised to break out of the sideways, most probably in the direction of the prevailing trend. It is therefore of critical importance to determine the direction of the prevailing trend. To do this, we add MA233

and MA55 to our chart. Figure 5.1 shows MA233 and MA55, with
MA55 above MA233. Also notice that both MA233 and MA55 are
pointing upward and this suggests that the trend is also up on the
lower time frame MA21. Therefore, we will assume that any
successful breakout is likely to be a bullish upside breakout. We
will still acknowledge downside breakouts should they occur, but we
will classify these as low-probability high-risk events; we will
therefore choose not to trade the bearish downside breakouts
when we perceive the underlying trend to be still bullish.

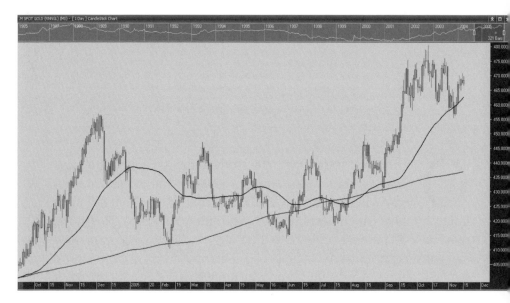

FIGURE 5.1   MA55 and MA233
Source: Reproduced by permission of *Market Analyst.*

We will now add MA21 and MA8. As a quick recap, we should be
able to quickly identify the type 1 trend pattern using MA21 as the
trending timeframe and trade trigger (Figure 5.2).

However in this chapter, our focus now is to identify and trade a
high-probability relatively low-risk breakout. We now assume that

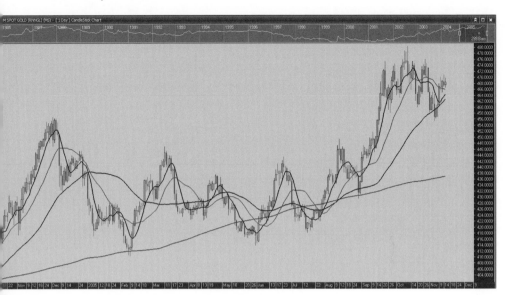

FIGURE 5.2 MA8 and MA21 with MA55 and MA233
Source: Reproduced by permission of *Market Analyst.*

any successful breakout should be a bullish upside breakout. The next step is to identify the sideways range.

Using a similar method from Chapter 1, we now identify peaks with a strength value of 8. This means that there are at least 8 candles on both sides of the peak candle. In Figure 5.3, we can define two peaks that we can use to determine a valid breakout.

Which shall we select as our significant peak? We can see that the market is in an expanded sideways range pattern, so the significant high is the dark solid line in Figure 5.3.

We will now insert the 60-period Average True Range. To recap, ATR60 measures the average size of the candles in our chart. In Figure 5.4, we can determine that the ATR60 has a value of 5.45.

In Figure 5.5, on the next candle, we observe that a bullish candle penetrated the intermediate dotted peak. This bullish candle had a range of 10.88 points. This is suggesting that the buying force is

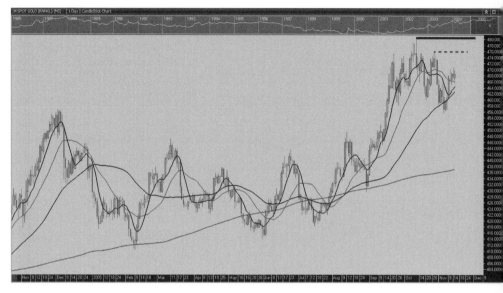

FIGURE 5.3 Identify sideways peak resistance
Source: Reproduced by permission of *Market Analyst.*

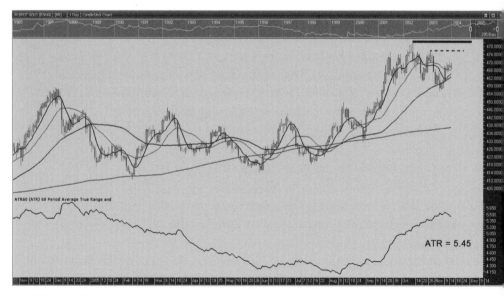

FIGURE 5.4 Insert the ATR60 tool
Source: Reproduced by permission of *Market Analyst.*

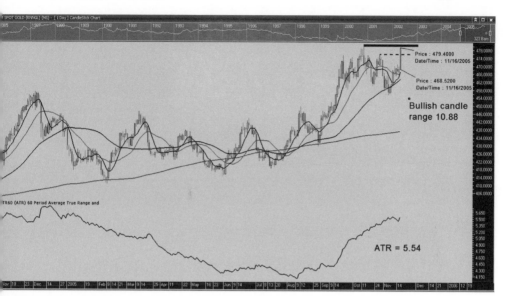

FIGURE 5.5 The intermediate breakout candle
Source: Reproduced by permission of *Market Analyst.*

significantly larger than normal. Notice that the ATR60 has also changed slightly, from 5.45 in Figure 5.4 to 5.54 in Figure 5.5.

This is an alert for us, as we can see that the buying forces are clearly displaying strength. Nonetheless, the market has not yet broken above the extended range ceiling. We need to monitor the potential breakout closely, and in Figure 5.6 we can see the breakout candle.

What can we observe about this breakout candle? First, it is a bullish candle, with a range of 9.22 points, and this breakout is in line with what we expect, given the context suggested by both MA233 and MA55. Second, the candle's range of 9.22 points is larger than the ATR60; in other words, the breakout candle has an above average range. This strongly suggests that the participants in this breakout have strength and commitment. There is also a third way to measure the "breakout power ratio." This mathematically compares the body of the breakout candle above the previous high (call this breakout A) to the body of the breakout candle below the previous high (call this breakout B). Figure 5.7 will show this process of calculating A as well as B. Breakout power is the ratio of A to B.

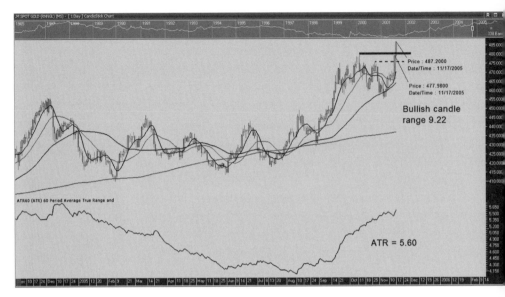

FIGURE 5.6 The breakout candle
Source: Reproduced by permission of *Market Analyst*.

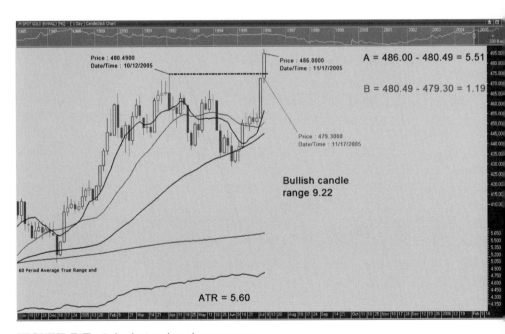

FIGURE 5.7 Calculating breakout power
Source: Reproduced by permission of *Market Analyst*.

In our example, the high of October 12, 2005 has a value of 480.49. The close of the breakout high day was at 486.00, and the opening of the breakout day was at 479.30. Therefore the value of the body of the breakout above the previous peak is 486.00 minus 480.49. We can now define the value of "breakout A" as 5.51. How do we calculate the value of "breakout B"? This is the part of the breakout candlestick's body that is within the expanded sideways range. We can take the value of the previous high and subtract it from the breakout candle's open. As the previous high has a value of 480.49, and the breakout candle opened at 479.30, the value of "breakout B" is 1.19. Therefore, the breakout power ratio is the division of "breakout A" by "breakout B". As "breakout A" has a value of 5.51 and "breakout B" has a value of 1.19, this breakout power ratio is calculated as the division of A (5.51) by B (1.19) giving a mathematical value of 4.63. This suggests that mathematically, the strength and commitment of the trending force is sufficiently strong to overcome the hurdles of the sideways range force. Think in these terms—if the breakout power is less than 1.00, what can we say about the strength and commitment of the breakout? We can assume that if the breakout power ratio is below 1.00, the sideways range is more likely to remain intact. What we wish to see as our qualification rules is that breakout power ratio is at least above 1.00, and this breakout candle must also be at least equal to the value of the ATR60.

We can see that in our example, this breakout candle has a range of 9.92, which is above the value of the ATR60 (5.60), and the breakout power ratio is also at 4.63, which is above our minimum requirement of 1.00. We now have high confidence that this breakout is likely to be a successful turtle-style, breakout trade. Using the *aikido* metaphor, we can now determine that the charge of the bulls is strong and is more likely to continue. It will therefore be wise not to oppose this bullish force. Indeed, the *aikido* principle is to now merge, blend and be with this buying force. To refresh and to anchor this metaphor into our memory, turn to page 13 and revisit the illustration "Be with the strong force" in Chapter 1.

Having this confidence is necessary if we intend to execute this turtle-style breakout trade. However, we must always remember that the market action after our entry must continue to give us confidence that our analysis is correct, and that our trade can succeed.

The first validation requirement is that the breakout momentum continues and does not stall. The range of the breakout candle represents the breakout momentum, and we will label the first candle of this breakout with a mathematical plus (+) sign (Figure 5.8).

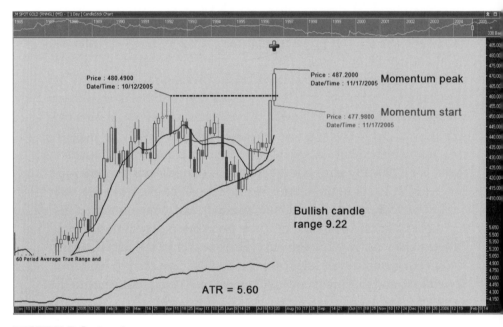

FIGURE 5.8 Breakout momentum
Source: Reproduced by permission of *Market Analyst.*

What we are looking for is the extension of the breakout momentum to suggest the success of the breakout. Therefore, any violation of the starting point of the breakout candle is cause for us to reconsider our view. Should this occur, we will label this violation with a mathematical minus (−) sign. Let us now proceed with the development of this example (Figure 5.9).

We now see that the momentum of this breakout has extended. In other words, the breakout force is still strongly charging ahead. The momentum start was not violated so there is no reason to label a mathematical (−) sign, but if the market does break below the momentum start, then we will have to label this event accordingly.

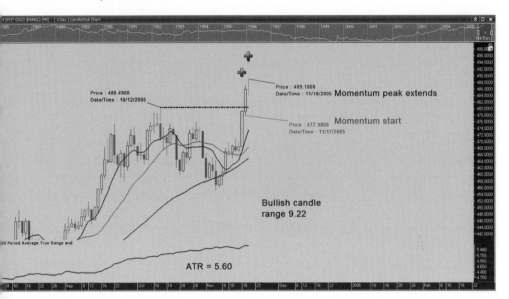

FIGURE 5.9 Breakout momentum continues
Source: Reproduced by permission of *Market Analyst.*

We calculate momentum as the summation of all the mathematical
(+) and mathematical (−) signs, and once we arrive at a net of
three mathematical (+) signs, we will acknowledge that the market
has the required momentum to proceed in its breakout attempt.
Figure 5.10 shows the ideal vision of how momentum is defined.
Notice that the momentum (+) signs were consecutive candles. It is
important to clarify that we can also accept non-consecutive momentum candles, as long as the momentum start is not challenged.

The prior sideways range was used to define the breakout level,
and therefore also defined the breakout bar. The second validation
requirement is to have the market display persistency. In a bullish
upside breakout, we need to see at least five consecutive candles
that are clearly above the prior sideways range, which is the breakout level. Put another way, after the breakout candle occurs, we
want to see that the market does not re-enter the previous sideways
range for a consecutive period of at least five candles. Indeed, we
want to see that the market stays clearly above the breakout level for
at least five candles (Figure 5.11).

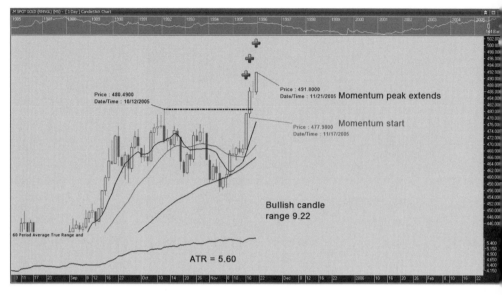

FIGURE 5.10 Breakout momentum is now validated
Source: Reproduced by permission of *Market Analyst.*

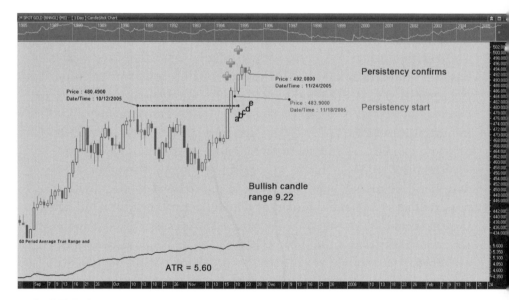

FIGURE 5.11 Breakout persistency is now validated
Source: Reproduced by permission of *Market Analyst.*

Let us go through the entire identification and qualification process.

Pre-Breakout Conditions and Action

1. Determine the trend of the market using MA55 and MA233. A bullish trend is assumed if MA55 is above MA233, and a bearish trend is assumed if MA55 is below MA233 (Figure 5.1). The direction of both MA55 and MA233 should also be pointing in the same direction in order to indicate the direction of the trend of the lower timeframe.

2. We will only consider breakouts that are in the direction of the trend.

   a. Identify a correction pattern. This can either be the extended sideways range pattern or the correction that occurs in a type 1 trend pattern. This identifies the breakout level (Figures 5.2 and 5.3).

3. We will monitor the market for the breakout when it approaches the breakout level. In a bullish market, the breakout is on the upside of the correction phase, and obviously, in a bearish market, we are looking for a downside breakout of the correction phase.

The Breakout Stage

1. Determine the ATR over 60 candles (ATR60).

2. Compare the breakout candle with ATR60 (Figures 5.4, 5.5, and 5.6).

3. Determine the breakout power ratio (Figure 5.7).

4. We will only accept and trade breakout candles that are at least as large as the value of ATR60 and also have a breakout power ratio of at least 1.00 and above.

Post-Breakout Validation Stage

Monitor the post breakout stage for the market to validate the breakout. There is a two-step process in the validation process:

1. Breakout momentum (Figures 5.8, 5.9 and 5.10).
2. Breakout persistency (Figure 5.11).

Trading the Breakout

We now have the process to identify whether the breakout is likely to succeed. We now need to structure a trade plan to trade the breakout:

1. Our entry trigger is on the close of the breakout candle that has been accepted by the breakout stage (Figure 5.12).

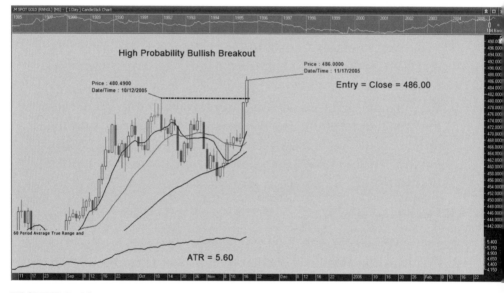

FIGURE 5.12 Breakout entry
Source: Reproduced by permission of *Market Analyst.*

2. We now need to calculate the stop loss. We do this by finding out the low of the breakout candle and then filter the ATR60 value below this low. What we are effectively saying is that we will recognize a probable expanded sideways range pattern if the market trades to our stop loss. In our example, the low of

the breakout candle is 477.98 and ATR60 has a value of 5.60. Therefore the stop loss will be set at 472.38 (Figure 5.13).

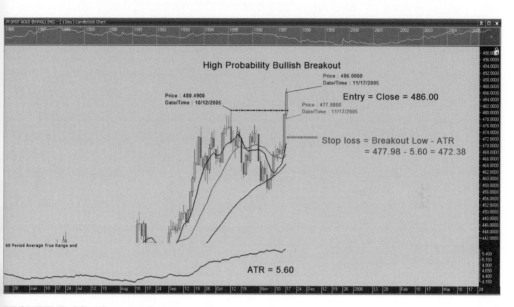

FIGURE 5.13 The stop loss
Source: Reproduced by permission of *Market Analyst.*

3. We now need to determine the expected loss of this trade. This is simply the difference between our entry and the stop loss. As our buy entry is at 486.00 and our stop loss is at 472.38, the expected loss is easily calculated with a value of 13.62 (Figure 5.14).

4. This is probably a good moment to revise what we have covered in Chapter 3 when we looked at the reward to risk ratio. We know that the formula for the break-even reward to risk ratio is based on the ratio of the miss rate to the hit rate of our method. We also know that the turtles have a well-documented statistical hit rate of 30 percent and a miss rate of 70 percent. Therefore, the break-even reward to risk ratio for the turtles is 2.33, and as we are now trading the breakout, we are trading like the turtles. We will therefore need to ensure that our reward to risk ratio is

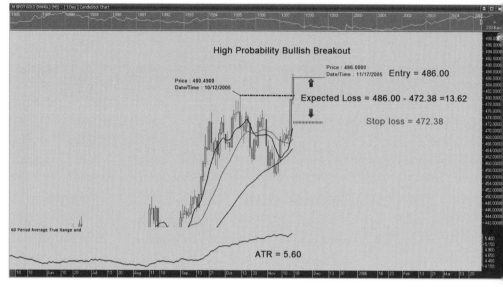

FIGURE 5.14 The expected loss
Source: Reproduced by permission of *Market Analyst.*

larger than 2.33 to trade successfully over time. Our trade plan
will use a reward to risk ratio of at least 2.80. With this in mind,
we can now calculate our expected profit, which will be the
expected loss multiplied by the reward to risk ratio of our trade
plan. Knowing the expected profit will then allow us to calculate
our profit target exit, and in our example we can plan for this
trade to give us an expected profit of 38.14. We calculated
this value by multiplying 2.80 by the expected loss of 13.62
(Figure 5.15).

The related procedure is now to calculate the exit level that
will give us this expected profit. This is simply the addition of
the expected profit to our entry level. We therefore can set
and draw our exit target by adding 38.14 to 486.00 to arrive at
524.14 (Figure 5.16).

5. Our trade plan will now require us to monitor the validation
   process. We will allow a time window of 13 candles for this

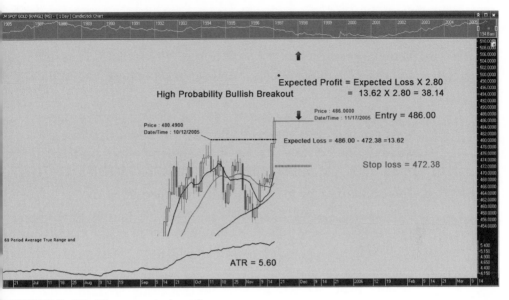

FIGURE 5.15 The expected profit
Source: Reproduced by permission of *Market Analyst.*

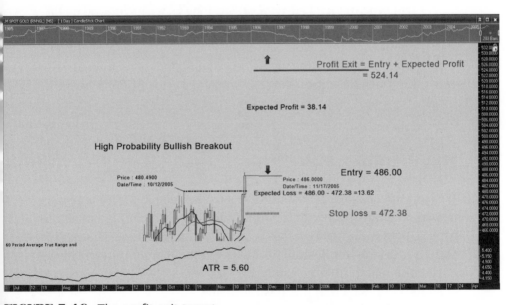

FIGURE 5.16 The profit exit target
Source: Reproduced by permission of *Market Analyst.*

validation process to take place. Here are the scenarios of what can occur after our trade entry candle:

a. The market shuts us out with a loss. We accept this result calmly; especially since we have pre-planned the trade in advance.

b. The market does not shut us out, but the validation process does not give us confidence after the 13-candle window. We will exit immediately. We may have either a minor profit or a minor loss. We will accept this as a possible outcome.

c. The validation process successfully completes on or before candle 13, and the market then gives us our desired exit target. This is our ideal result, which we will also accept calmly.

d. The market reverses after a successful validation and shuts us out. Again, we will also accept this result as part of the process of dealing with uncertainty. Probability theory states that a single trade result can be random, but the overall result will be statistically driven, and as long as we have good quality statistics of the system that we are trading, we can have confidence that wins and losses will be part of a continuing stream of trades that we will encounter and that our result over time will be reflected in the statistical edge of our system.

MANAGING THE TRADE

We have now engaged the market in a trade, and have a trade plan to manage the uncertainty of the future. We have a clear plan of action to exit if the market reverses against us, and also a clear action plan to exit with our desired profit should the market perform as we have anticipated in our analysis. Our example shows scenario (Figure 5.17), which is our desired result.

We will now look at an initial good, qualified breakout in the direction of the prevailing moving average trend. However, this

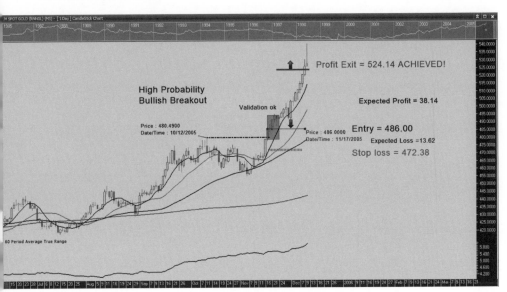

FIGURE 5.17 The market action agrees with our analysis
Source: Reproduced by permission of *Market Analyst.*

bearish breakout was not validated by momentum (Figure 5.18). Note that the two mathematical (+) signs denote the momentum of the breakout on the downside, and therefore the two mathematical (−) signs mark the reversal back into the extended sideways range. The two (+) and the two (−) signs means that the initial momentum has been lost. This short position should be immediately exited if it has not yet been shut out, precisely because the expected bearish trend continuation did not occur.

In *aikido* parlance, the strength of our opponent is suspect, and we therefore need to quickly disengage from combat because our original assessment is now showing signs of being incorrect.

We have now completed the basic stage in our journey to the land of market understanding. Let us review what we have discovered so far.

In Chapter 3, we concentrated on understanding how markets can behave in what we have called the extended sideways range

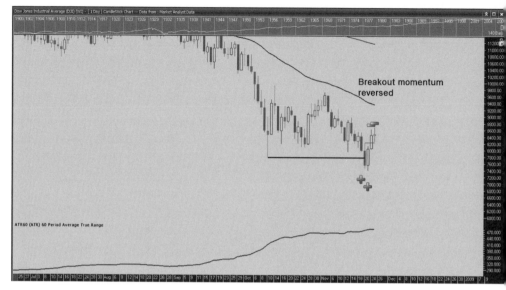

FIGURE 5.18 Non-validated breakout
Source: Reproduced by permission of *Market Analyst.*

pattern. This is akin to learning a first basic martial arts *kata*, or movement, and the more we practice it, the more fluent our understanding and execution will become. Our aim at this stage is to search for, understand it, and practice trading this pattern.

In Chapter 4, we focused specifically on the type 1 trend pattern. This pattern broadens our understanding of how markets can behave. Again, we now have a second basic *kata* that adds to our knowledge, and with increased knowledge we can develop and hone the skills to trade under two different market conditions, namely, the expanded sideways range, and the correction phase of the type 1 trend pattern.

In Chapter 4, we shifted our focus to zoom in on the breakout phase, which is where and how the market transits from the correction sideways range to the impulse trend mode. This is our third *kata* that completes the foundational aspects of market behavior. We will need to understand all three *kata*, not only on the mental abstract level, but also internalize this understanding through actual physical practice so that we can act with smoothness and precision under the stress of combative trading.

The underlying principle behind the *aiki* trading method is to locate what we can call "action zones." These action zones offer potential low-risk high-probability trading opportunities. We need to cultivate the patience to wait for these action zones to be correctly set up; once this occurs, we need to be very decisive in the execution of the trade entry.

The military analogy is to study a sniper. Snipers are usually well concealed as they very patiently wait for their prey to appear within their field of fire. Once the target appears in this high-probability low-risk target zone, the sniper decisively acts. There is also a more ancient precedent that we can refer to as our martial metaphor. Kenshin Uesugi was a famous *daimyo* who lived in 16th century Japan. He was apparently assassinated by a *ninja* who hid in a cesspit, patiently waiting for Kenshin to visit the latrine. Kenshin was duly stabbed with a short spear when he was in what he thought to be a private, secure, and safe spot! This incident tellingly illustrates three important principles. First, winning *aiki* trader picks his time and place of combat, when his method tells him that odds are in his favor. Second, the successful trader must adopt the mindset of the *ninja* assassin, who was prepared to do whatever it takes, including hiding in the cesspit, to achieve his goal. Finally, we must always be alert to both opportunities, and also for potential danger. Like the *ninja*, we need to patiently wait for opportunity, and then decisively strike when the opportunity presents itself. We also need to learn from Kenshin's fatal mistake: that we need to be alert at all times, as danger can arise unexpectedly.

One crucial component of success is our desire and motivation. We must truly desire success. Only with true desire will we be able to overcome the difficulties and setbacks that we will encounter in our journey. This group is much more likely to join the elite small minority who succeed and achieve their vision and goals. Unfortunately, those who are not truly motivated will allow these obstacles and setbacks to impede and cut short their progress. These are the people who will give up, and join the vast majority who do not achieve their goals.

We will end this phase of our journey with a famous quote attributed to Musashi Miyamoto, a 17th century master of the sword. What he said applies to both martial arts and the art of trading.

> *It will seem difficult at first, but everything is difficult at first! With time and practice, it will all become clear!*

If we have true desire and motivation, then Musashi's quote can encourage and spur us toward our goal of trading success.

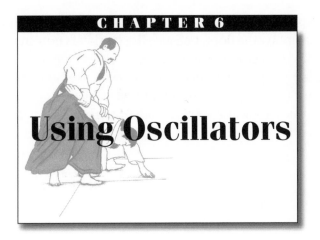

CHAPTER 6

Using Oscillators

W e now have some understanding of the two basic forces that control all market behavior. These two forces can be said to be in compression, or in expansion. When the market is in compression, we can expect the sideways range, which is one aspect of the correction or compression phase. The expansion force results in a trending phase when the market moves in distinct large impulsive expansions with minor small corrections.

In this chapter, we will look at some oscillators that enhance our view as to whether the prevailing mode is likely to continue or change. This is a very important upgrade in our knowledge, and has ramifications on how we will trade.

Let us say that we have defined a sideways range. If we have confidence that the sideways range is likely to continue, then our trading stance will be set. We can search for buy opportunities at the floor or hunt for selling opportunities at the ceiling precisely because we have confidence that the sideways range mode is likely to persist. But if we have the view that the sideways range is about to morph into an expansion impulse, then it will not be to our advantage to sell the ceiling or buy the floor, because the market is now more likely to break out of this compression phase. We can then select either the breakout strategy, or we can choose to await a temporary correction to search for a value zone to initiate our trade.

We will now look at Wilder's Relative Strength Index (RSI) and how we can use RSI to enhance our understanding of market behavior.

RELATIVE STRENGTH INDEX

The Relative Strength Index (RSI) was originally designed as an overbought–oversold indicator. Think of this oscillator as a pendulum that swings from one extreme (overbought or too high) to another extreme (oversold or too low). The original concept was to sell when the market is deemed to be too high because the buying strength can fizzle out, and to buy when the market is deemed to be too low, which is where sellers are expected to weaken. The martial arts principle still holds, and will then be applied: buy when the enemy seller is weak, and sell when the enemy buyer is weak.

There is a wealth of material that can explain how RSI is calculated and plotted. However like the *samurai*, we are more concerned with how to use the sword and less with how it is constructed. We will focus on how we can specifically use RSI to assist in answering the all-important question: Is the market mode likely to continue or likely to change?

We will start off with a 14-period RSI, and we will specifically amend the over-extended zones from the original 70 and 30 (Figure 6.1), to 60 and 40 (Figure 6.2).

In Figure 6.1, RSI is used as an overbought and oversold oscillator. We can observe that the traditional approach does not present us with any satisfactory understanding.

We now turn to Figure 6.2. We have set the one horizontal line at 60, and the other horizontal line at 40. The RSI itself fluctuates and can oscillate from between 0 and 100.

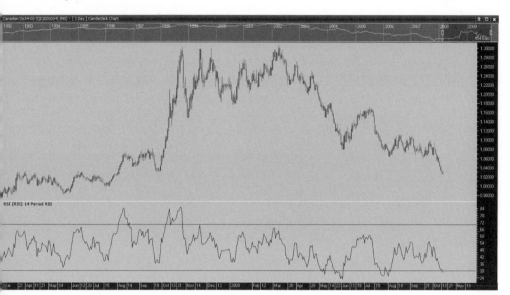

FIGURE 6.1 Traditional RSI with 70/30 setting
Source: Reproduced by permission of *Market Analyst.*

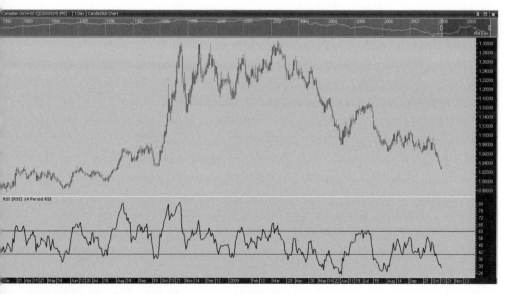

FIGURE 6.2 Modified RSI with 60/40 setting
Source: Reproduced by permission of *Market Analyst.*

What can we say about the strength of the buyers when RSI points upward, crosses and then stays above the 60 line? The acceptance above RSI-60 suggests that the buyers are strong, and that the market is in a bullish impulse with higher highs to come later (Figure 6.3). This is a very important observation and we will test this observation with different markets and timeframes.

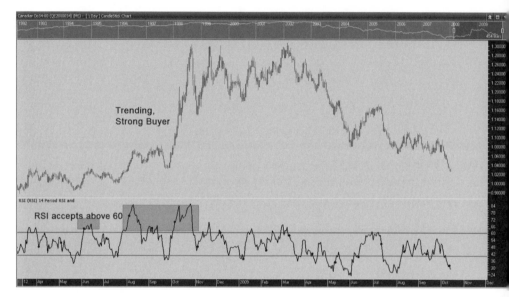

FIGURE 6.3 RSI indicating buying strength
Source: Reproduced by permission of *Market Analyst.*

The next important observation is to look at the correction phase. In a bullish trend, the correction must be caused by some counterattack by selling forces. Now, as long as the trend is still bullish, we will expect the correction to be weak. Notice that the RSI at the 40 line tends to "halt" the correction.

We can therefore hypothesize that RSI can be used as a measurement of strength. Strong, impulsive buyers are associated with RSI above the 60 line, and in a correction, the sellers are weak and RSI will tend to halt the weak sellers at the 40 line. We can link the corrective RSI concept to the *aikido* technique of entering directly against a weak opponent.

We now look at a bearish market where the strong impulses are pointing down and the weak corrections are pointing up. An impulsive bearish force must be the result of selling strength, and selling strength can be measured by a downward pointing RSI that drops and stays below the 40 line (Figure 6.4).

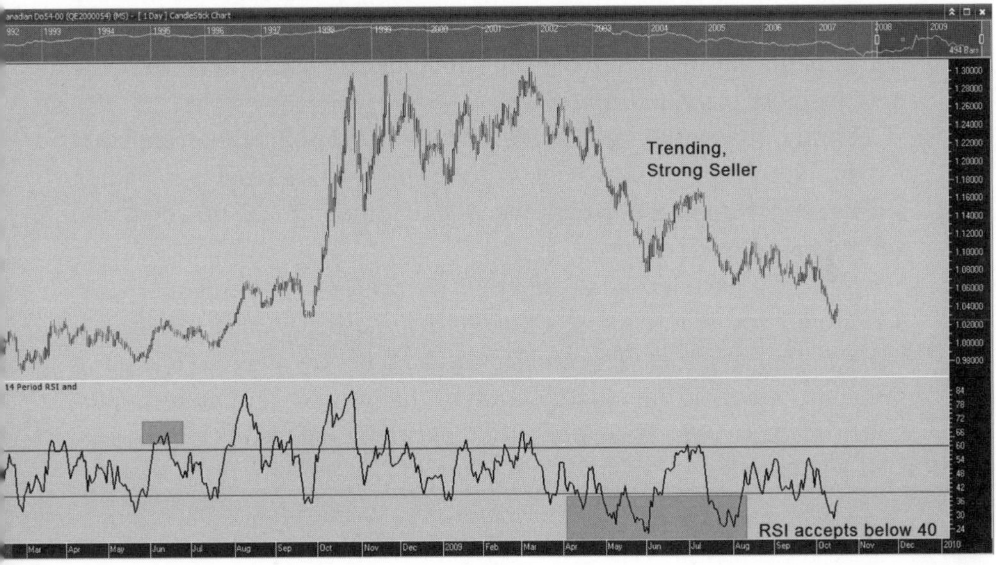

FIGURE 6.4 RSI indicating selling strength
Source: Reproduced by permission of *Market Analyst.*

What can we also say about the strength of buyers in the bear market rally? We can conclude that the buying force will have to be weak in a temporary correction, which characterizes the bear market rally. RSI will display this characteristic as an upward moving RSI that tends to halt at the 60 line.

Let us recap our observations in a tabular format.

Bullish market in up impulse mode	RSI up, accepts above 60
Bullish market in correction mode	RSI down, stays above 40
Bearish market in down impulse mode	RSI down, accepts below 40
Bearish market in correction mode	RSI up, stays below 60

8 bars above
7 bars or less bars below 40
8 bars below
7 bars or less above 60

The RSI can therefore enhance our market understanding and increase our confidence in our trading. The martial arts principle still holds true: buy when the enemy seller is weak; sell when the enemy buyer is weak. If the enemy is strong, do not resist, but merge.

RSI can now tell us whether the market is likely to be weak or strong, and therefore assist us in deciding whether to attack the weak force, or to merge with the strong force. Let us now integrate our existing knowledge from the previous three chapters with the new insights provided by RSI.

Firstly, we always need to identify the trend of the timeframe that we intend to trade. Knowledge of the trend will then set our trading stance. In a directional trend, we will be buyers in an uptrend, and sellers in a downtrend.

Next, we have to decide whether we prefer to patiently and conservatively respond to a correction, or to impatiently and aggressively react to the breakout. The conservative style now has the RSI parameters to assist in the identification of the impulse and more importantly, also the correction phase of the directional trend (Figure 6.5).

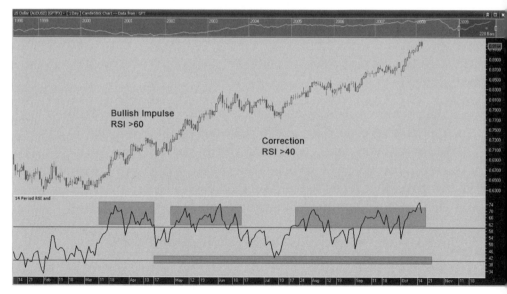

FIGURE 6.5 RSI action in bullish trend
Source: Reproduced by permission of *Market Analyst.*

Once we have the view that the market in Figure 6.5 is in bullish impulse, the conservative trader can insert a moving average (either MA8 or MA21) to identify the type 1 trend pattern. This trading setup, or *kata*, can provide us with one potential entry trigger. The conservative trader can also stay alert for the expanded sideways range pattern, which can also provide another potential entry trigger. Remembering that the impulsive mode is bullish, we intend to take the buy side of the expanded sideways range pattern (Figure 6.6). Using these RSI parameters, the aggressive breakout trader can also hunt for breakout trades that match the rules that we discussed in Chapter 5.

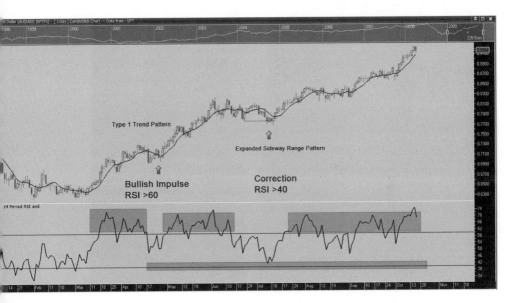

FIGURE 6.6　RSI suggests sideways correction low in a bullish market
Source: Reproduced by permission of *Market Analyst*.

In Figure 6.7, the RSI parameters suggest that the trend is bearish. The process of learning any skill involves practice. Perhaps we can use this example to look for trade setups that will trigger our short trades. What are the patterns that we currently know? How do we identify these patterns? How do we look to trade these patterns?

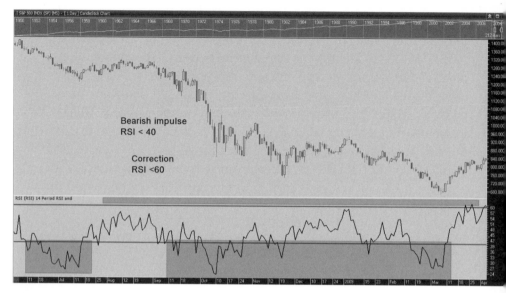

FIGURE 6.7 RSI action in bearish trend
Source: Reproduced by permission of *Market Analyst.*

If we can locate these patterns and entry setups in Figure 6.7, then we will improve our ability to spot the same patterns in other charts that we will be looking at in the future. Remember, the key to success in both martial arts as well as in trading is to practice, practice, and do more practice!

THE RSI DIVERGENCE SIGNAL (OR RSI CAMOUFLAGE SIGNAL)

In Chapter 5, we learnt that we can use moving averages to assist us in trend determination. The position of MA55 in relation to MA233 will suggest to us whether the market we are examining is in a bullish or bearish phase.

We now turn our attention to Figure 6.8. We can see that MA55 is below MA233, and this suggests that the higher time frame trend is bearish. However, we can argue that between March 17, 2008 and

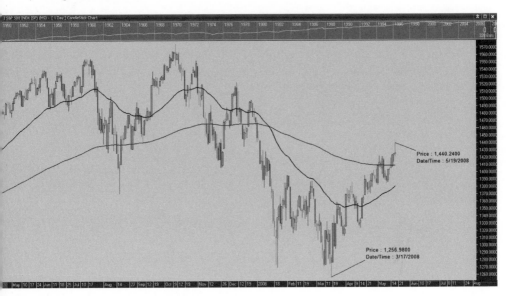

FIGURE 6.8 Bearish higher time frame
Source: Reproduced by permission of *Market Analyst.*

May 19, 2008, the market traded with higher highs and higher lows. During this period, we can therefore say that the shorter-term trend was bullish. With MA55 below MA233, the higher timeframe bias suggests that this is more likely to be a correction and not the start of a new uptrend.

Let us now insert our RSI. Figure 6.9 shows that the RSI crossed above the 60 line. We have to acknowledge that RSI now suggests that buyers are at present apparently looking strong. But is there any additional information that we can glean from the RSI? Look at the RSI value on May 2, 2008, and compare this to the RSI value on May 19, 2008. We can see that the RSI value on May 19 is lower than the RSI value on May 2. Now, we understand that RSI is a tool that can measure strength, and above the 60 line, we are measuring buying strength. Now let us associate the buying strength with the actual market price.

On May 2, RSI buying strength was 64.29 and on the same candle, the market high was 1422.72.

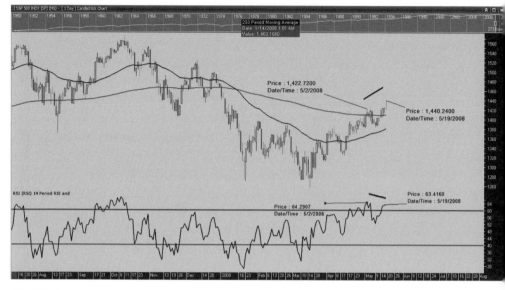

FIGURE 6.9 RSI in divergence
Source: Reproduced by permission of *Market Analyst.*

On May 19, RSI buying strength was 63.41 and on the same candle, the market high was higher at 1440.24.

The RSI has now detected an anomaly. The market has traded higher, but RSI did not register greater strength as would be normally expected. This particular configuration is known as the RSI divergence and in this case, is suggesting that the higher high seen on May 19 is actually accompanied by a weaker buying force as compared to the previous high of May 2. While the market can still continue upward, the RSI divergence suggests that the market is more likely to stall and reverse, as the internal strength of the market is actually weak.

The martial arts principle is to attack when your enemy is weak, and as the buyers are now expected to be weak, we will attack as the seller. We will search specifically for a pattern that can trigger our sell entry, and the expanded sideways range pattern suggests an entry when we see a bearish candle (Figure 6.10).

The market in this case proceeds to validate our analysis, and rewards us with a profitable trade (Figure 6.11).

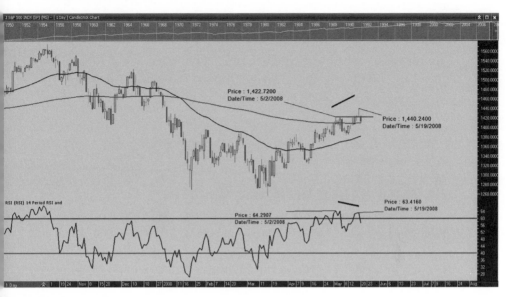

FIGURE 6.10 RSI in divergence: initiating the trade
Source: Reproduced by permission of *Market Analyst*.

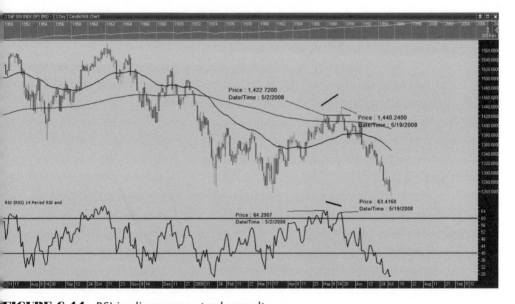

FIGURE 6.11 RSI in divergence: trade result
Source: Reproduced by permission of *Market Analyst*.

There is one very important condition that we will need to consider when we are looking at RSI divergence. This divergence signal must be within 14 candles, precisely because our RSI is configured to calculate relative strength over the past 14 candles. We cannot be looking for divergence over periods that are beyond the setting of our RSI.

THE SLOW STOCHASTIC OSCILLATOR

Developed by George C. Lane in the late 1950s, the stochastic oscillator is a momentum indicator that shows the location of the current close relative to the high/low range over a set number of candles.

There are two ways that we can use the slow stochastic oscillator. The traditional method is to employ it as an overbought/oversold oscillator. This is only useful when the market is in a sideways range mode. Typically, when the stochastic is at high values above 80 the market, then proceeds to sell off, and when the stochastic dips below 20, the market quickly stages a rally.

The second and preferred way of interpreting the stochastic oscillator is to observe whether it is consistently above 80. This indicates that buying forces are in control and that the market is likely to be in an impulse and in a bullish trend. Conversely, if the stochastic oscillator consistently accepts below 20, this indicates that selling forces are in control, and that the market is in a bearish trend impulse.

Figure 6.12 shows the 14-candle slow stochastic oscillator in a bullish directional up trending market. The slow stochastic oscillator crosses above, and then stays above the stochastic 80 level to indicate a bullish impulse. This is highlighted by the shaded rectangles. As we have set our slow stochastic to be calculated over a 14-candle period, we will qualify acceptance above 80

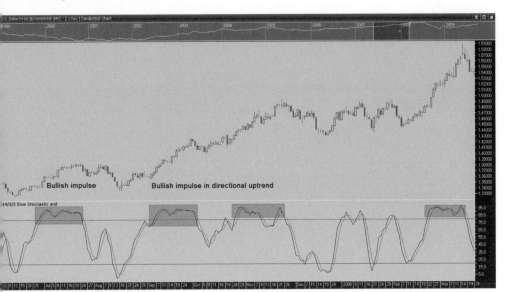

FIGURE 6.12 Slow stochastic action in bullish impulse
Source: Reproduced by permission of *Market Analyst.*

to mean that at least eight consecutive candles show stochastic readings above 80. The longer it stays above 80, the stronger is the impulse.

Once we have the presence of a strong buying force, we know that our action should be to join the buying forces. We can choose to buy when there is a weak counter attack by sellers. Can the slow stochastic pinpoint this opportunity?

Well, we also know that the slow stochastic oscillator can act like a pendulum, swinging from overbought to oversold conditions. In a bullish trend, the end of the correction is typically marked by the slow stochastic at values below 20. We expect this selling to be weak, and therefore we can expect the stochastic to stay below the 20 line for only a short period. As a rule, we will qualify a correction in a bull market if the stochastic oscillator trades below 20 for less than seven candles. The shorter the time it stays below 20, the stronger the corrective view becomes (Figure 6.13).

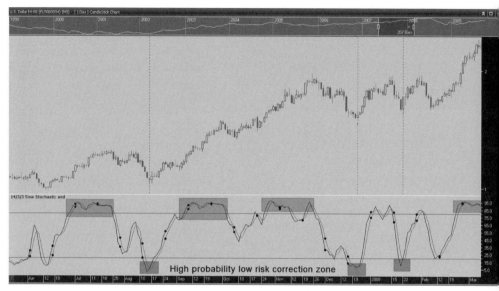

FIGURE 6.13 Slow stochastic action in bullish correction
Source: Reproduced by permission of *Market Analyst.*

We can tabulate this observation thus:

Bullish trend in impulse mode	Slow stochastic accepts above 80
Bullish trend in correction mode	Slow stochastic rejects below 20

In a bullish trend, we may also decide to trade high probability bullish breakout signals. The stochastic oscillator must be already displaying a trend pattern, and the breakout must also be accompanied by a stochastic reading above 80. The stochastic oscillator then accepts above 80 to enhance our view that the trend is bullish (Figure 6.14).

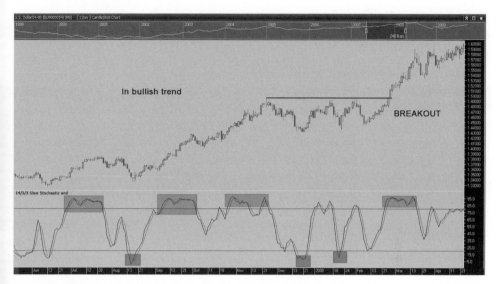

FIGURE 6.14 Slow stochastic action in bullish breakout
Source: Reproduced by permission of *Market Analyst.*

We can now add to our table the observation for the bullish breakout condition:

Bullish trend in impulse mode	Stochastic above 80 and accepts
Bullish trend in correction mode	Stochastic below 20 and rejects
Bullish trend in bullish breakout	Stochastic above 80 and accepts.

If the stochastic can be used to identify a bullish trend, we can also expect it to identify a bearish trend. We can expect the bearish conditions to fit the following table:

Bearish trend in impulse	Stochastic below 20 and accepts
Bearish trend in correction	Stochastic above 80 and rejects
Bearish trend in bearish breakout	Stochastic below 20 and accepts

Figure 6.15 illustrates the slow stochastic oscillator performing in a bearish market. We can see that the behavior fits our table.

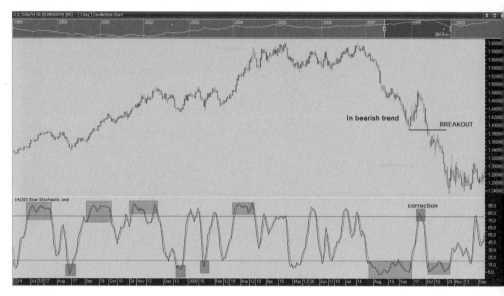

FIGURE 6.15 Slow stochastic action in bearish trend
Source: Reproduced by permission of *Market Analyst.*

The martial arts philosophy tells us that if the enemy is weak, counterattack strongly. If the enemy is strong, do not oppose, but turn and merge with the enemy.

In trading, if the trend is bullish (RSI accepts above 60, or slow stochastic accepts above 80), we can await temporary weakness and then enter strongly when the selling force dissipates (RSI above 40 or slow stochastic rejects 20).

If the trend is bearish (RSI accepts below 40, or slow stochastic accepts below 20), we can await a temporary rally and then enter strongly when the weak buyers fade away.

Once the trend can be established, we can choose to also trade the breakout in the direction of the underlying trend. This means that we are turning and merging with the strong force.

In this chapter, we have seen how the RSI and slow stochastic oscillators can be used to enhance our understanding of the underlying trend. These oscillators also help us identify the price and time zone where we should be hunting for a trade. To initiate the trade, we need to see a candlestick pattern that moves in the direction that we anticipate. Some useful candlestick patterns we can look for are the single-candle shooting star or hammer patterns, the two-candlestick dark cloud cover, piercing candle patterns, or engulfing candles, in addition to the turtle soup expanded sideways range pattern we discussed in Chapter 3.

Let us now practice using both RSI and slow stochastic in our analysis and trade. We will set both RSI and slow stochastic to calculate their respective values over a 14-candle period. Remember, if RSI crosses and accepts above 60, we assume that the market is in a bullish impulse and that the subsequent trend to also be bullish. Slow stochastic also accepts above 80 and both oscillators are in alignment (Figure 6.16).

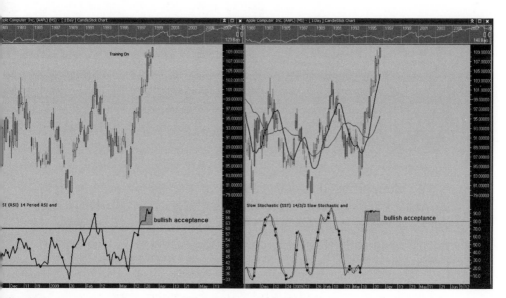

FIGURE 6.16 RSI and slow stochastic in bullish action
Source: Reproduced by permission of *Market Analyst.*

If we are aggressive, we can elect to trade with the success-ful breakout method discussed in Chapter 5. If we choose to be cautious, we will await a correction, identify when the correction is likely to fade, and enter at a relatively superior value. What do we expect to see? We expect that RSI should not accept below 40, and that the slow stochastic should quickly bounce off the 20 zone (Figure 6.17).

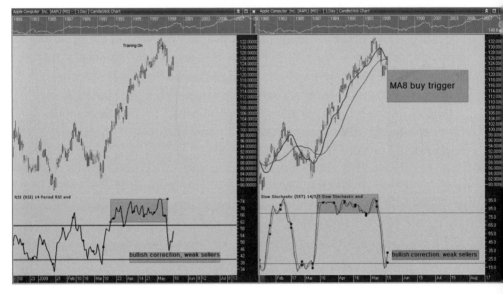

FIGURE 6.17 RSI and slow stochastic action
Source: Reproduced by permission of *Market Analyst.*

We then proceed with the MA8 type 1 trend pattern buy signal and calculate our stop loss and exit target. Let us recap what we have learned so far and do this exercise. What information do we need to perform the calculation of the stop loss and the profit exit?

1. We will need to find out the value of ATR60.
2. We need to find out the value of the swing low of the correction.

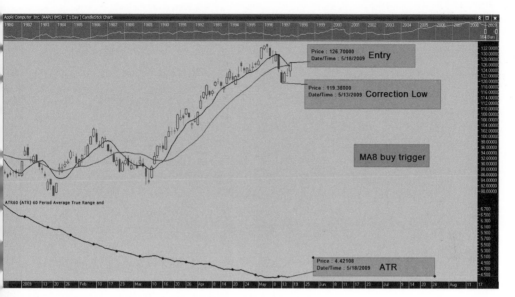

FIGURE 6.18 Trade planning: the entry
Source: Reproduced by permission of *Market Analyst.*

3. We also need to know our entry price.
   Figure 6.18 shows us that:
   - ATR60 has a value of 4.42;
   - the swing low on May 13, 2009 was at 119.38, and
   - our entry price was 126.70 on May 18, 2009.
4. The stop loss is the correction low filtered by the ATR60. Mathematically, this is 119.38 minus 4.42, giving the stop loss as 114.96.
5. The expected loss is the difference of the entry and the stop loss. Mathematically, this is 126.70 minus 114.96, giving an expected loss of 11.74.
6. Therefore the expected profit is 1.80 times the expected loss and we derive the value of our expected profit as 21.13.
7. Our expected exit price is then the entry plus the expected profit. This works out to 147.83 (Figure 6.19).

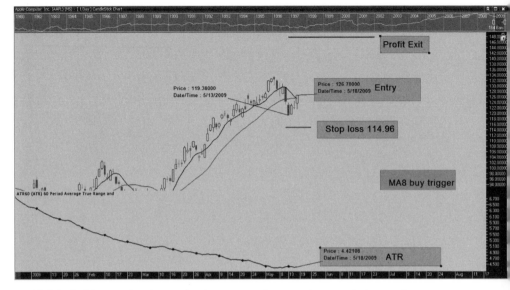

FIGURE 6.19 Trade planning: the entry, the stop loss and the profit exit
Source: Reproduced by permission of *Market Analyst.*

We have analyzed the market and have planned a trade based on our understanding of market behavior. We have accepted the possibility of loss, and have confidence that our profit objective can be met (Figure 6.20).

Once the trade is closed out, we will need to reassess the trend and repeat the hunt for the next low-risk, high-probability trade entry. This will give us opportunities to practice our analysis and our trade planning skills. The more work and effort we put in, the more experience we will gain. We can expect that over time we will become more and more competent in our trade analysis, planning, and execution.

In the military and in martial arts training, the beginner is guided and taught in a highly structured and regimented manner, in the belief that the more the beginner sweats in training, the less he will bleed in battle. The beginner trader unfortunately does not have a drill sergeant or a *sensei* to enforce discipline, so those who truly wish to succeed must either engage a good and conscientious

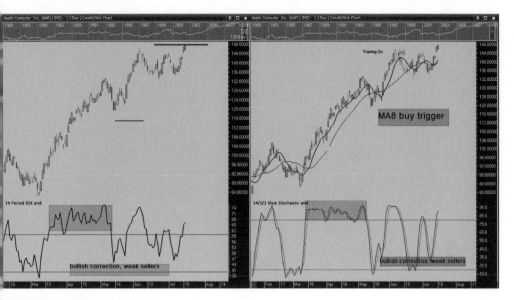

FIGURE 6.20 The result
Source: Reproduced by permission of *Market Analyst.*

trading coach or mentor, or they need to put in much more effort in self discipline. This is easier said than done. Again, we need to know our vision and goal, so that when the going gets tough, we have a real reason to continue. Without this guiding light, the majority of us as self-directed traders will easily give up in the face of difficulty and adversity.

CHAPTER 7

Applying Fibonacci Numbers and Ratios in Trade Analysis

We began our journey with the study of the expanded sideways range pattern, and then continued with the type I trend pattern and the successful breakout pattern. Essentially, the type 1 trend pattern is closely related to the successful breakout pattern, as both are part of the same market structure. To recap, the expanded sideways range pattern has a series of almost equal highs and lows, whereas the type 1 trend pattern has a relatively large impulse and a visibly smaller correction. This is the key distinguishing feature marking the difference between these two patterns.

By using oscillators like 14-period RSI and the 14-period slow stochastic, we can enhance our understanding of the market's intention. We know that in a directional up impulse, RSI-14 should stay above the RSI-60 level for at least eight candles, and that the correction when it occurs should halt near the RSI-40 level. In a directional down trend, the bearish impulse will stay below the RSI-40 level for at least eight candles, and the subsequent rally halts near the RSI-60 level.

Is there any other tool we can employ to locate a quality correction zone?

Also, our initial profit exit strategy is based on the reward to risk ratio. Is there a tool that we can use to give us a superior exit strategy based on market structure and market behavior?

One such tool we can now look at is the Fibonacci sequence of numbers and its related ratios.

The Fibonacci sequence starts with two integers, zero and one. The next integer number in the sequence is the sum of the previous two numbers:

0, 1.
0, 1, 1.
0, 1, 1, 2.
0, 1, 1, 2, 3.
0, 1, 1, 2, 3, 5,
0, 1, 1, 2, 3, 5, 8, 13, 21, 34, 55, 89, 144, 233.

The moving averages that we have used are actually Fibonacci numbers that approximate certain time periods on the end of day chart. The eight-day moving average represents approximately the trend of the weekly timeframe. The 21-day moving average represents approximately the trend of the monthly timeframe. The 55-day moving average represents the trend of the quarterly timeframe and the 233-day moving average represents the trend of the yearly timeframe.

In trading, the important and relevant Fibonacci ratios we will use are:

0.312
0.500
0.618
1.00
1.618
2.618

These Fibonacci ratios are divided into two groups, either below 1.00 or from 1.00 and above. The ratios that are below 1.00 are used to determine correction zones. Remember, we know that a correction

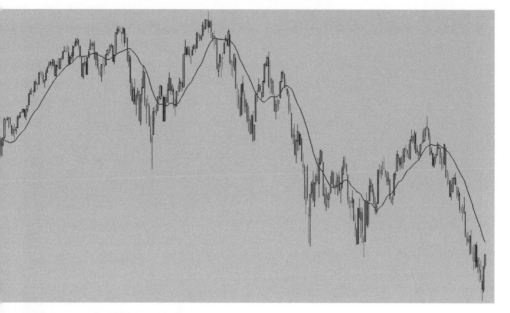

FIGURE 7.1 Identifying the impulse
Source: Reproduced by permission of *Market Analyst.*

comes after an impulse. Therefore, the first task is to identify and label the impulsive move. Let us now examine Figure 7.1.

This chart is a daily closing chart, and has a 21-day simple moving average. A cursory examination shows that MA21 is currently pointing down, and has lower lows and lower highs. We can deduce that in the monthly time frame this market is trending down.

We will now add into our chart RSI-14 to give us enhanced information about the prevailing trend (Figure 7.2). We can visually see that RSI has stayed below the RSI-40 line for more than the minimum required eight days. This strongly suggests that we are witnessing a *bearish impulse.*

This bearish impulse started when the previous correction ended. We can locate the previous correction by the upward curve of MA21. We will label the start of the impulse as "X" and we will also label the current low as "A?" (Figure 7.3). Why do we use the question mark in our labeling? The simple answer is that "XA" is the impulse movement, and as long as there is no correction in this timeframe,

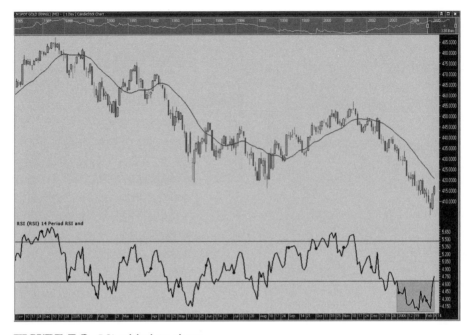

FIGURE 7.2 RSI added to chart
Source: Reproduced by permission of *Market Analyst.*

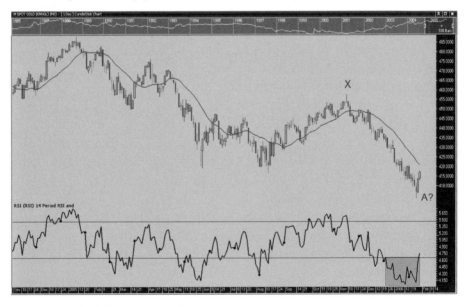

FIGURE 7.3 Label the impulse
Source: Reproduced by permission of *Market Analyst.*

then the impulse has not yet ended and can actually continue. We can only confirm the impulse after we see a recognizable correction in our timeframe. At this point, the market is still in impulse.

We now progress to Figure 7.4. Here we see that the candlesticks have started to cross above MA21, and also that MA21 is beginning to curve upward. This signifies that the market in this timeframe is probably in its correction phase. We expect to see RSI ideally staying below the RSI-60 level during this correction. However, we will allow for a temporary penetration above the RSI-60 line as long as this penetration is for less than seven candles (i.e., six candles is the most we will allow). As we are now looking at a potential upward correction in the bear market, we can confirm our XA bearish impulse, and now label our correction as "B?" because the correction may still continue. So far, what we have done is based on what we have covered previously in the chapter on the type 1 trend pattern, and in the chapter on the RSI oscillator.

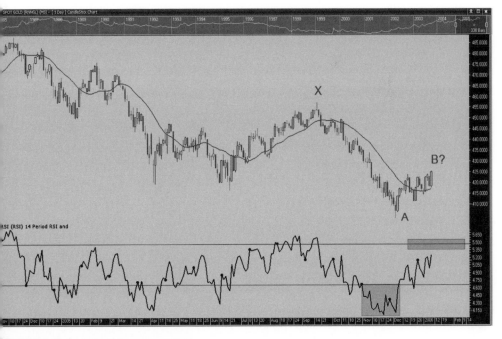

FIGURE 7.4 Label the correction
Source: Reproduced by permission of *Market Analyst.*

We expect the correction to be smaller than the impulse, therefore the ratio of the correction to the impulse must be less than 1.00. In Fibonacci theory, there is a mathematical relationship between the size of the correction to the size of the impulse. Mathematically, we can express this relationship as AB/XA = the Fibonacci retracement ratios.

The Fibonacci retracement ratios that we will use are:

0.382;
0.500; and
0.618.

This means that as long as we know the value of the impulse XA, we can easily calculate an ideal zone where we can anticipate the termination of the correction. We can see that the market is entering the ideal correction zone, as defined by the use of the Fibonacci retracement ratios (Figure 7.5).

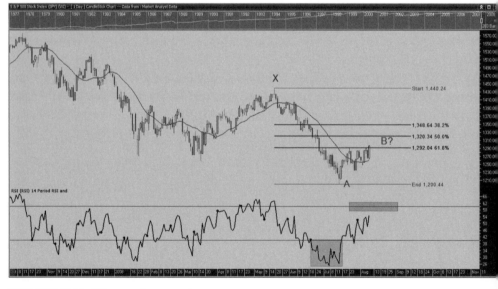

FIGURE 7.5 Fibonacci correction zone
Source: Reproduced by permission of *Market Analyst.*

The type 1 trend pattern will mechanically trigger an initiating sell trade once the market closes, in this case, below MA21. Using the Fibonacci retracement ratios can fine-tune our potential entry zone, and we can await a directional candlestick to enter our trade. In this example, let us review the confluence of signals that suggests the end of the correction and also the trade entry.

1. RSI below the RSI-40 level suggests a bearish impulse. We label the impulse as XA?.
2. The correction kicks in. We see MA21 curving upward, and the market trades from below MA21 to above MA21. However, this buying force is weak as seen in the RSI halting before the RSI-60 line. We therefore label the impulse wave as XA, and the correction wave as AB?.
3. We have inserted the Fibonacci retracement and we can see that the retracement ratio of AB to XA is within the ideal Fibonacci retracement relationship.
4. The turtle soup bear bar can initial our trade as we now can anticipate the start of the next impulse. The market is in a type 1 trend pattern, but our new tools have given us enhanced confidence, and also allowed us to hunt for a superior entry signal by selecting the sideways expanded range pattern, which is also humorously known as the turtle soup entry.

Once the trade is done, we need to determine the exit for both the stop loss as well as for the profit target. Let us continue with our checklist:

Stop loss (Figure 7.6):

Insert ATR60 and determine its value;

Calculate stop loss

　　Stop Loss = (B? high) plus (value of ATR60)

　　Stop Loss = 1313.15 + 22.60 = 1335.75.

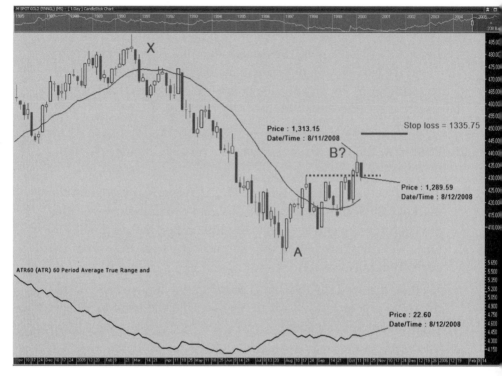

FIGURE 7.6 The stop loss
Source: Reproduced by permission of *Market Analyst.*

Reward to risk profit target (Figure 7.7):

1. Calculate expected loss;
   a. Expected Loss = Stop Loss Entry
   b. Expected Loss = 1335.75 − 1289.59 = 46.16.
2. Calculate expected profit;
   a. Expected Profit = 1.80 times Expected Loss
   b. Expected Profit = 1.80 × 46.16 = 83.09.
3. Calculate the reward to risk exit target;
   a. Exit target = Entry Expected Profit
   b. Exit Target = 1289.59 − 83.09 = 1206.50.

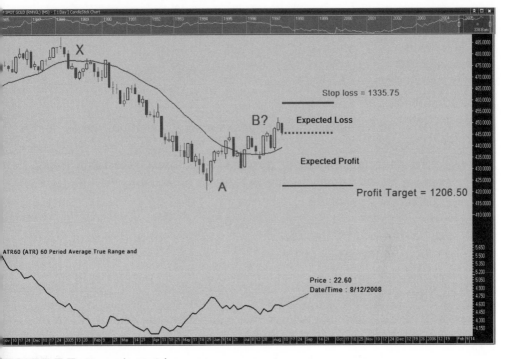

FIGURE 7.7   Reward vs. risk
Source: Reproduced by permission of *Market Analyst.*

ASSESSING THE FIBONACCI PROFIT TARGET

So far, what we have seen is the use of a set of Fibonacci ratios to determine the relationship of the AB correction wave to the XA impulse wave. Fibonacci theory also states that there is a relationship between the initial XA impulse wave and the continuation impulse BC, which is how we will label the impulse wave that we now expect to be in. In a perfect world, the perfect relationship is 1.00. This means that the XA impulse will be exactly equal to the BC impulse. However, we are all trading in an imperfect world, so we use Fibonacci expansion ratios to suggest potential target levels for profitable exits.

The Fibonacci expansion ratios are:

0.618
1.000
1.618
2.618.

We can visualize these targets as small, medium, large, and extra large.

To determine the target C? we need to know the size of the initial impulse XA. We then say that BC should be equal to the Fibonacci expansion ratios of XA.

1. Therefore if BC impulse is small, we can expect the size of BC to be equal to 0.618 of XA.

2. If the BC impulse is medium, we can expect the size of BC to be equal to 1.000 of XA.

3. If the BC impulse is large, we can expect the size of BC to be equal to 1.618 of XA.

4. And if the BC impulse is extra large, we can expect the size of BC to be equal to 2.618 of XA.

We now refer to Figure 7.8. We have labeled the start of the bearish impulse as X and the end of the bearish impulse as A. We have also labeled the end of the rally correction as B. In Figure 7.8, we have also calculated our stop loss exit as well as our reward to risk profit target.

The Fibonacci expansion tool can now assist us in drawing the Fibonacci profit targets. The Market Analyst 6 software requires us to select the Fibonacci expansion tool, and firstly click on X, the start of the impulse. Next, we click on A, the end of the impulse. Finally, we click on B, the possible end of the correction, which is also the possible start of the next impulse. The Fibonacci targets will then be automatically calculated and displayed on our chart. In our example, the first Fibonacci target we see is the small target (Figure 7.9). The medium and large targets have been drawn, but the chart scale does not as yet allow us to see this.

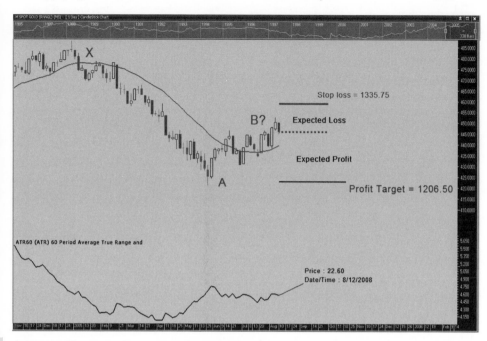

FIGURE 7.8 Impulse XA and correction AB
Source: Reproduced by permission of *Market Analyst.*

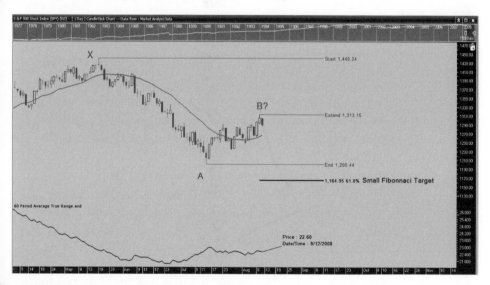

FIGURE 7.9 The "small" Fibonacci target
Source: Reproduced by permission of *Market Analyst.*

The market then proceeds to move, and in this case, the analysis turns out to be correct and the market rewards us with a profit at the small Fibonacci target (Figure 7.10), and then eventually achieves the medium and large Fibonacci targets (Figure 7.11).

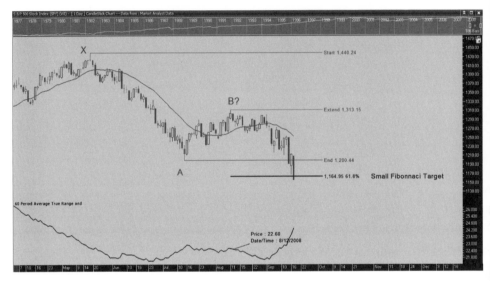

FIGURE 7.10 Reaching the "small" Fibonacci target
Source: Reproduced by permission of *Market Analyst.*

It is important for us to practice as much as possible on our own. Remember, the more we practice the better we will become. It is important that we recognize the errors that we make in the learning process, and as we continue with our practice, we will avoid the initial mistakes and hone our understanding and execution of the correct techniques.

Let us start our practice session by looking at Figure 7.12.

What do we need to do? Perhaps it is best if we can follow a checklist, just like martial arts practitioners follow a set of movements, or *kata*.

1. What is the trend of the longer-term moving averages? We use MA55 and also the MA233 (note that we use the exponential moving average for the higher timeframes). We observe that:

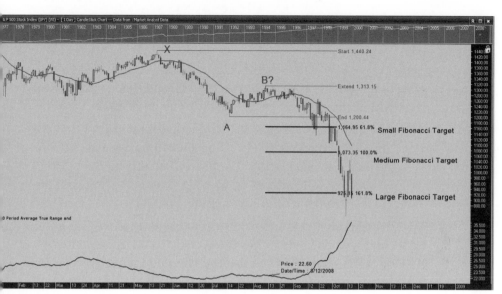

FIGURE 7.11 The "medium" and the "large" Fibonacci target
Source: Reproduced by permission of *Market Analyst*.

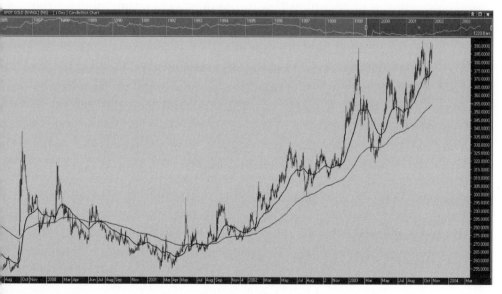

FIGURE 7.12 Practical training: higher timeframe perspective
Source: Reproduced by permission of *Market Analyst*.

    a. MA55 is in a trend pattern, with higher highs and higher lows.

    b. MA233 is pointing upward.

    c. In other words, MA55 is above MA233, and this configuration is within the context of an upward bias in MA233.

        i. We can conclude that the lower timeframe trend that we intend to trade is likely to be bullish so we can set our strategy in line with the prevailing strong buy force. Therefore, our stance is to be a buyer. We will initiate all our trades with a buy action.

2. We now look at the shorter term timeframe that we intend to trade, and we can trade either the weekly trend, represented by MA8 or MA21 (note that we use the simple moving average for the lower timeframes.). For the purpose of this exercise, we will elect using MA21 as our preferred trend and timeframe.

3. What is the trend of MA21?

    a. We can observe a higher high and a higher low pattern and this is in accordance with the perspective suggested by the higher timeframe moving averages.

4. Is this uptrend likely to continue?

    a. We will insert the 14-period RSI (Figure 7.13). We believe that bullish impulses should accept above RSI-60 and that in temporary declines, the RSI-40 should indicate the end of the selling dip.

        i. We conclude that in Figure 7.13, we recognize a high probability type 1 trend pattern.

        ii. The type 1 trend pattern entry is the close above the 21-period SMA.

5. We need to label the impulse, and the correction (Figure 7.14).

    a. We then insert the Fibonacci retracement levels to give us greater confidence that the market is in a high probability correction of a directional trend.

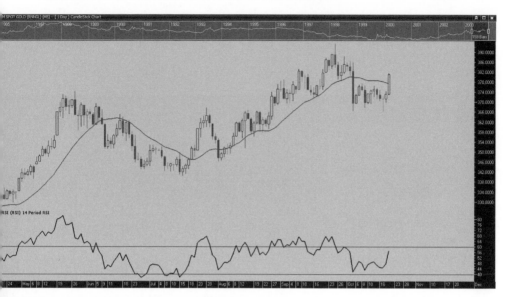

FIGURE 7.13   Practical training: add RSI
Source: Reproduced by permission of *Market Analyst.*

FIGURE 7.14   Practical training: add labeling
Source: Reproduced by permission of *Market Analyst.*

6. We then calculate this trade's stop loss exit and also the reward risk profit exit. To do so, we need some information (Figure 7.15):

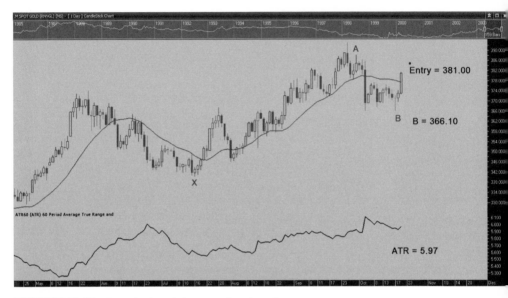

FIGURE 7.15 Practical training: trade planning
Source: Reproduced by permission of *Market Analyst.*

    a. The value of the 60-period ATR. (5.97).

    b. The B swing low (366.10).

    c. The entry price (381.00).

    d. What is the price of the stop loss? If we do the calculation correctly, we should arrive at this answer (360.13).

    e. What is our profit exit level? Use this opportunity to practice. If we do not get the correct result, (418.57), it will tell us that we will need to know why and where we made the error, and therefore we can learn and improve on our technique and our craft.

7. Next we will determine the Fibonacci exit targets and compare this with the reward to risk exit target (Figure 7.16).

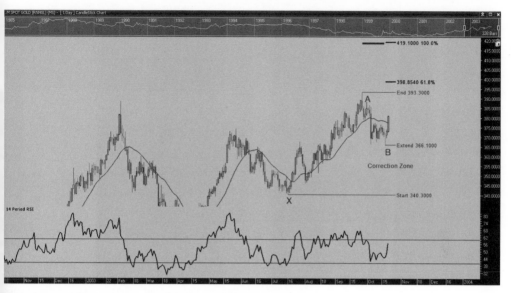

FIGURE 7.16 Practical training: Fibonacci targets
Source: Reproduced by permission of *Market Analyst.*

    a. We know that our reward to risk exit target is 418.57. There-
fore, we will ignore the small Fibonacci target and elect to
exit at the medium Fibonacci target.

  8. We then patiently wait for the market to either reward us with a
profit, or to stop us out with an acceptable loss at our predefined
stop loss level. In this case, the market performed as we
expected and we duly exited at our predefined profit target
(Figure 7.17).

In this chapter, the important points that we must understand
and internalize are that the Fibonacci retracement ratios provide us
with a quality retracement zone, and that the Fibonacci expansion
ratios suggest high probability exit targets. It is crucial that we elect
the target that best fits our reward to risk exit.

Remember, continued and sustained practice will improve our
understanding of the market, and also our execution of the trade

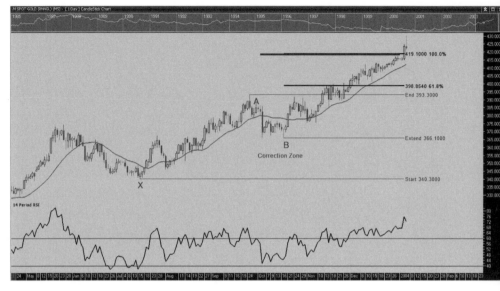

FIGURE 7.17 Practical training: trade conclusion
Source: Reproduced by permission of *Market Analyst.*

plan. It requires us to put in the necessary time, effort, and energy to perform the analysis. In order to do this analysis, we need to invest in the required tools and data so that proper analysis can be performed.

Perhaps it is a good moment to discuss how the human mind functions, as this understanding may assist us in handling the innate difficulties that block the majority from achieving their stated goals and desires. We already know that the human psyche will try its utmost to avoid pain, and will very easily gravitate toward pleasure. Recent research has shown that the human mind associates effort and work with pain and discomfort. The human brain is also very much attuned to immediate pleasure, and is less able to accept present discomfort and present pain, for future reward and future pleasure. This is why so many resolutions and good intentions remain unfulfilled, primarily because of the way our minds work. Perhaps this knowledge will forewarn and prepare us. This is where the dedicated practice of martial arts can inculcate this necessary mindset. In martial arts terms, this ability to accept present pain for future pleasure is known as "eating bitter" and practicing this philosophy will assist the *aiki* trader in his journey to the destination of trading success.

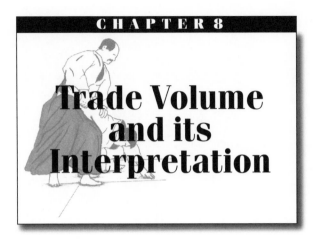

CHAPTER 8

Trade Volume and its Interpretation

So far, all our analysis has been based solely on price behavior, as represented by Japanese candlestick charting. We can enhance our understanding of what the market is saying if we also know how to listen to the clues provided by the trade volume.

Let us recap our understanding of Japanese candlesticks and what they try to portray. The start of the trading period (weekly period, daily period, or hourly period) is like the initial contact of swords. The thrust, counterattack, and riposte will finally determine the winner at the end of that trading period. The winner can either be the bullish force traditionally drawn with a white or unshaded candle body, or the bearish force, which is traditionally depicted as a black, filled-in candle body. In addition, the distance between the open and the close of combat will show the strength of that period's winning force, and the total distance traveled reveals the range between the high and the low Figure 8.1.

Let us now consider the information provided by the volume of transactions during this trading period. The best analogy we can

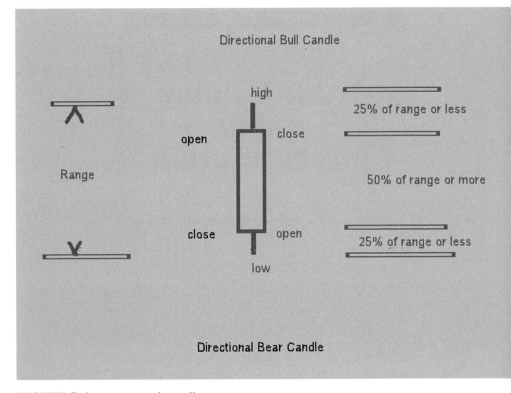

FIGURE 8.1 Directional candles
Source: Reproduced by permission of *Market Analyst.*

use is to think of this volume as the energy that feeds and fuels this contest between the combating forces. It will be normal to expect that a high-volume or high-energy period should result in a directional candlestick, which can be either bullish or bearish.

Let us now revisit the principles we discussed when the market is in the expanded sideways range. At the sideways ceiling (or resistance top) we can expect the buying forces to be weak, so candlestick patterns at the ceiling or resistance should confirm the strength of the sellers and the weakness of the buyers. Conversely, at the sideways floor (or support bottom) we can anticipate the buying force to be strong, and the selling force to be weak.

We recollect that when the market breaks out of the sideways range pattern, there is a 70 percent chance that the breakout is false. This sets up what we call the turtle soup trade.

Let us now consider what the transaction volume can suggest to us. Transaction volume represents the net total commitment and interest of the market combatants, and we can think of volume as the fuel that provides energy to the market. When the market is performing a breakout, what will low volume suggest? It will suggest that the breakout attempt is half-hearted, and that there is no true commitment in the breakout participants. In other words, a breakout with low volume is like an attempt to overcome an obstacle without sufficient energy, and without sufficient energy, this breakout attempt is likely to fail.

On the other hand, if the breakout attempt is accompanied by a higher transaction volume, then we can infer that the breakout force is strong, committed, and aggressive. We can also imagine that the high volume provides the necessary fuel to energize the continued assault of the obstacle, be it resistance or support.

Let us start by looking at the expanded sideways range and then add in transaction volume to enhance our analysis (Figure 8.2). We note that the market is approaching the swing low of August 16,

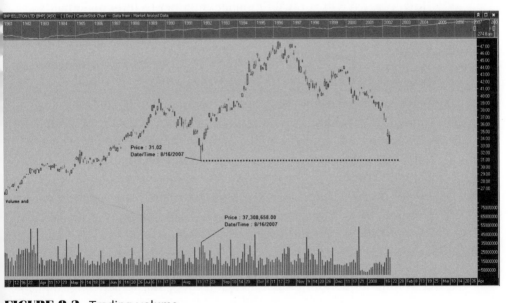

FIGURE 8.2 Trading volume
Source: Reproduced by permission of *Market Analyst.*

which is denoted by the dotted horizontal support line. We know that on this previous low of August 16, the market staged a significant upward move, so this swing low should represent buying support. We also know that the transaction volume on August 16 was 37.308 million shares traded.

Let us now think about the three possible scenarios as the market price approaches this support. The market may almost, but not quite, reach the $31.02 support line and begin to rally; the market can touch this line exactly and rally or the market may break out, in this case, below the $31.02 support line, and thereafter either embark on a new bear trend impulse or revert into the expanded sideways mode.

Let us consider the breakout scenario. A breakout is the attempt by sellers to overwhelm the buying forces that previously defended the $31.02 swing low.

1. If we see a breakout with volume significantly less than 37.308 million, we can infer that the breakout attempt by sellers is unconvincing and lacks commitment and also lacks energy. However, we will apply a Fibonacci number to filter and qualify the breakout volume. *We will define a breakout volume at least 3 percent lower than the volume at the previous support or resistance as "significantly lower." This volume rule will enhance the expanded sideways range view.*

2. If we see a breakout with higher volume significantly greater than 37.308 million, we can then assume that the breakout attempt by sellers is genuine and committed. However, we will apply a Fibonacci number to filter and qualify the breakout volume. *We will define a breakout volume at least 8 percent higher than the volume at the previous support or resistance as genuine and "significantly higher." This volume rule will enhance the successful breakout attempt.*

On January 22, the market traded to a new low of $31.00, on a lower volume of 28.413 million shares traded. Mathematically, this breakout volume is 23.8 percent less and is therefore a significantly

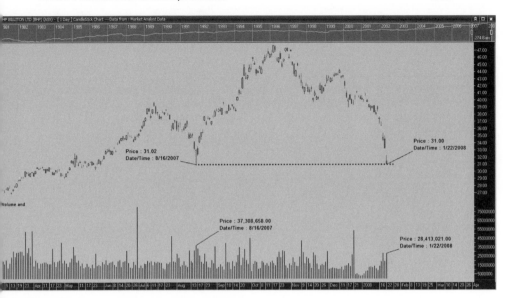

FIGURE 8.3 Comparing breakout volume
Source: Reproduced by permission of *Market Analyst.*

lower volume. Based on the volume rule, we perceive that the selling force is not as strong as the buying force that previously defended the $31.02 level. In other words, we perceive that the selling force lacks the energy to continue strongly down, despite the true range directional bear candle breakout. This leads us to suspect that the market is most probably still in the extended sideways range. We can enter a buy trade if a bullish candle appears. Notice that the turtle soup buy signal was accompanied by a higher volume, compared to the volume of the bearish breakout candle. This tells us that the breakout attempt to breach the support had weak selling energy, but the counterattack in the turtle soup buy signal had higher energy than the selling attempt. Nonetheless, even though our confidence in this trade may be high, we will as usual, filter and place our stop loss below the new low (Figure 8.4).

We know that in any sideways market, the price will tend to rotate between the floor and the ceiling. More importantly, the expanded sideways range suggests that we have a 70 percent probability of

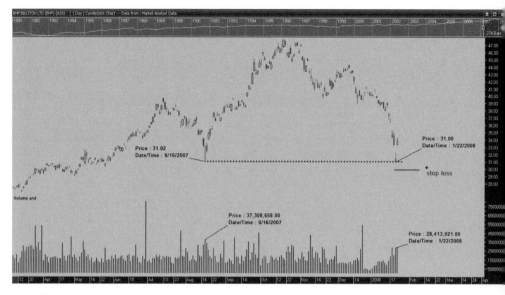

FIGURE 8.4 The stop loss
Source: Reproduced by permission of *Market Analyst.*

succeeding. The inclusion of this particular volume configuration further increases our probability of success. The market in this case validates our view, and the market now approaches the ceiling (Figure 8.5). From the chart, we can see that the market is now approaching the ceiling resistance high of $47.70, which was achieved on October 18. This resistance is marked by a dotted line.

Our data also shows that at the October 18 peak, 17.093 million shares were traded.

We can anticipate three possible scenarios. The first scenario is that the market approaches but does not exceed the $47.70 high. The second scenario is that the market touches the $47.70 high exactly and reverses direction. The third scenario is that the market breaks above the $47.70 high. The quality of the breakout candle and the transaction volume on this candle will give us the necessary information to assess whether the breakout is genuine or whether the expanded sideways range is still the operating mode.

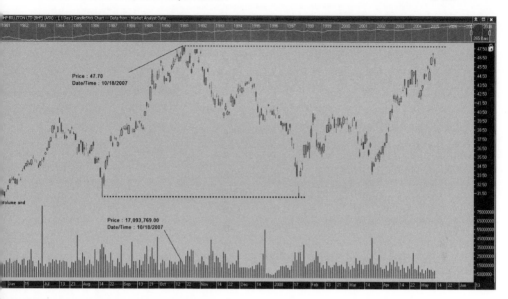

FIGURE 8.5 Approaching the target
Source: Reproduced by permission of *Market Analyst.*

What kind of volume do we expect to see if the breakout is genuine? Well, we expect to see a bullish candle with transaction volume significantly above 17.093 million shares. If this occurs, we will have confidence that the buying force not only control the breakout day, but that the interest and commitment of the buying force is greater than the previous selling peak. We can visualize high volume as the fuel that will energize the breakout charge above the resistance.

On the other hand, if the breakout transaction volume is significantly below 17.093 million shares, we can then infer that the breakout is likely to fail, and that the expanded sideways range is still in control.

We have now envisaged possible scenarios, and we will be prepared for whatever this market can do. In this case, the market breaks out with a bullish candle, with a transaction volume of 17.817 million shares traded (Figure 8.6).

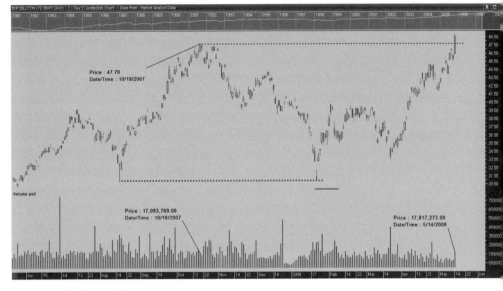

FIGURE 8.6 Breakout again
Source: Reproduced by permission of *Market Analyst.*

Numerically, we can say that the transaction volume is larger,
but let us review the numbers again. The volume on the breakout
candle is 17.817 million and on the previous high, the volume was
17.0993 million. Mathematically, this works out to be only 4.23
percent higher, and therefore fails the Fibonacci qualification. We
therefore suspect and question the validity of the breakout, as the
volume rule suggests that the breakout attempt is, at best, uncertain
and indeterminate, because this breakout volume is neither considered as significantly larger, nor significantly smaller (Figure 8.7). We
will therefore elect not to trade the bullish breakout attempt.

We will now combine the various tools and methods that we
have diligently studied and practiced. In Figure 8.8, we have added
MA55 and MA233. We have also inserted RSI-14.

These are our observations:

1. MA55 is pointing down, suggesting that the lower timeframe
   trend is bearish.

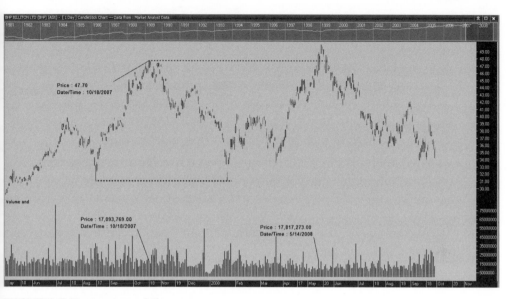

FIGURE 8.7 Breakout fails
Source: Reproduced by permission of *Market Analyst.*

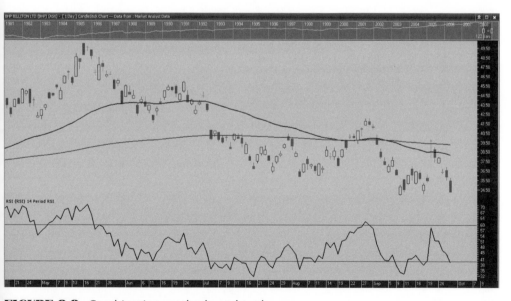

FIGURE 8.8 Combination methods and tools
Source: Reproduced by permission of *Market Analyst.*

2. MA55 is below MA233. This suggests that the bearish trend is likely to continue.

3. RSI-14 is very clearly showing that the up moves are corrective in nature, and the down moves suggest some acceptance below RSI-40. This enhances our bearish view and suggests that we should initiate new trades with a "sell first, buy back later" strategy. This is also known as a "short sell" strategy.

4. We can choose to sell with the type 1 trend pattern, by waiting for a temporary market rally, or we can elect to use the break-out strategy.

We now insert the volume data into our chart (Figure 8.9) and observe the following:

1. The sideways low on September 10 was at $33.90. The market subsequently rallied, so this low represents a strong buying force.

2. The transaction volume on September 10 was 25.249 million shares traded.

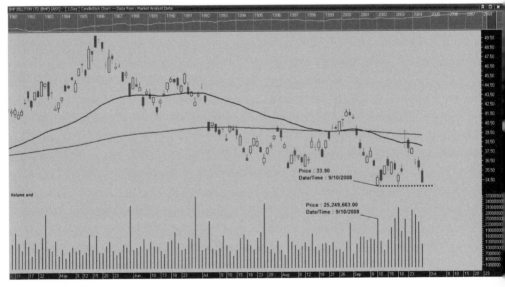

FIGURE 8.9 Insert volume analysis
Source: Reproduced by permission of *Market Analyst*.

Let us consider the successful breakout scenario. Under this scenario, we are looking for candlestick breakout power, and the breakout volume should be significantly larger. The Fibonacci rule will require the breakout volume to be at least 1.08 times 25.249 million shares. So we are looking for a breakout bar with breakout power larger than 1, and also a breakout volume larger than 27.269 million shares. On September 30, the market gaps down with a volume of 31.660, and closes at the low (Figure 8.10).

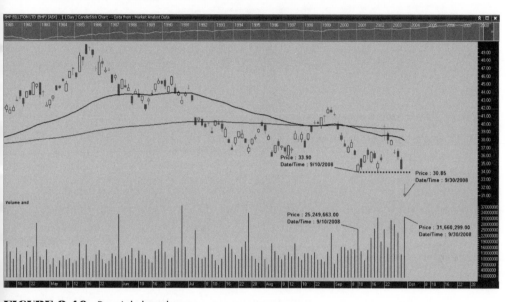

FIGURE 8.10 Bearish breakout
Source: Reproduced by permission of *Market Analyst.*

The breakout power is larger than 1, and the breakout volume qualifies this as a high probability successful breakout. The market then proceeds to sell off (Figure 8.11).

The analogy that compares volume to energy can also assist us in understanding some crucial principles. Let us consider a high-volume high-energy trading period, which can be a weekly, a daily, or even an hourly candle. It is normal to expect high volume and high energy to result in a directional candle, which can either be bullish or bearish. However, there will also be occasions where high volume

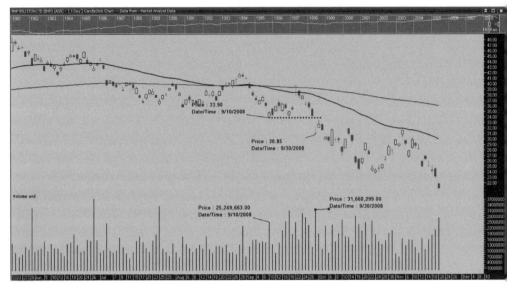

FIGURE 8.11 Successful breakout
Source: Reproduced by permission of *Market Analyst.*

and high energy produces a below average, indeed a subnormal candlestick range. To recap, the candlestick range is the distance that the combating forces travel, and if high energy is applied but the distance covered is relatively small, then one obvious reason is that there is an obstacle that is impeding and countering the high energy that is being fed into the candlestick. This obstacle may be caused by the higher timeframe chart meeting its resistance or support. The competent *aiki* trader must be alert to the subtle clues provided by volume. Remember the advice of Sun Tzu, to "know the enemy." In trading, the external enemy is the market. Every successful trader must understand market behavior, and the better we can understand how the markets behave, the better our chances of success in trading.

Let us review and list the salient points of this chapter. We are specifically looking for a sideways range market. As the market probes the upper ceiling resistance and the lower support floor, there will be attempts by the directional trending force to break out of the sideways pattern. We will use the clues provided by the transaction volume to assist us in answering the all-important question: Is the sideways range likely to continue or is the sideways range likely to change into a directional trend impulse? Obviously, the answer to this question will set our trading strategy.

If the sideways range mode is likely to continue, we can sell near the top, and buy near the bottom of the identified sideways pattern. We will sell when the buyer weakens and we will buy when the seller weakens.

If the sideways range mode is changing into a directional trend impulse, then we need to consider merging with the new impulse. In a successful upside breakout we will merge with the buyers. In a successful bearish breakout, we will merge with the sellers.

Let us now review the conditions and rules that will help us to answer the all-important question when the market is probing the sideways top and bottom.

1. As the market approaches a sideways top (or bottom), we wait for the market to break out above (or below) the previous high (or low) of this sideways pattern.
2. We need to determine the value of that high (or low), and also the transaction volume of that candle.
3. When the market breaks out above the old high (or below the old low), we will determine the breakout power of the break-out candle.
4. We will compare the volume of the breakout candle to the volume at the previous high (or low).

We conclude that the sideways range mode is likely to continue if the breakout power of the breakout candle is less than 1 and the transaction volume at the breakout is significantly lower than the volume at the previous swing. The filter we use is a 3 percent filter. This means that if the previous volume is 100 million shares traded, then we expect the sideways range mode to prevail if the breakout volume is 97 million or less.

We also can conclude that the successful breakout is more probable when the breakout candle has a breakout power larger than 1, and the transaction volume of the breakout candle is significantly larger than the volume at the prior swing. We define significantly higher as at least 8 percent higher than the previous volume. This means that if the previous volume is 100 million shares traded, then a successful breakout is more likely if the breakout candle records a volume of at least 108 million shares or more.

In the case of a directional market, we will recognize potential danger when we see high-volume trading accompanied by a below-average candle range. This is a subtle clue that higher timeframe forces are at play, and these higher timeframe forces are absorbing the high-volume energy feeding into the market and limiting the size of the lower timeframe candle.

In some financial markets, especially the unregulated foreign exchange market, which is traded over-the-counter or OTC, an accurate transaction volume may not be available. We will generally only get accurate volume data from regulated exchanges. Some of these regulated exchanges (for example the Chicago Mercantile Exchange) trade in futures contracts that have a defined lifespan. If we look at any of the volume data when the contracts expire, we will notice a spike in the volume. This occurs at every expiry period and is caused by traders exiting their expiring contracts and then re-entering their position in the fresh or front contracts. This distinctive characteristic of futures markets makes volume analysis complicated, as we will need to find ways to statistically "normalize" the regular spikes in the volume.

This problem is less likely to occur in equity markets. We will therefore only use volume analysis on regulated stock exchanges, and we will prefer to limit our analysis to the top 100 capitalized shares as technical analysis works best with freely traded large markets.

Risk, Money, and Trade Management

THE LEARNING PHASE

Over the past eight chapters, we have learned some basic and robust aspects of market behavior. Essentially, the market we are looking to trade will either be in a directional or expansion mode, or in a sideways or contraction mode.

We have adopted the strategy of trading in the direction of the current market mode, as long as our tools suggest that the current market mode is likely to continue. This means that in a directional uptrend where the prevailing force is pushing the market price higher, we will merge with the strong buying force. Our method allows us to either hunt for a low-risk buy when:

1. The market temporarily corrects (the type 1 trend pattern);
2. The market allows us to buy in an extended sideways range pattern; or
3. The market performs a successful breakout.

153

Obviously, in a continuing directional downtrend, we will be looking to join the prevailing strong selling force.

In a continuing sideways mode, we can elect to trade with the expanded sideways range pattern.

When we initially start putting these trading setups into practice, we should be trading with the minimum trade size that is applicable for the market that we are in. This is important because as beginners we are expected to make errors, either in our understanding or in the execution of the various methods discussed in the previous eight chapters. Can we expect errors to be generally profitable? Well, that is unlikely, as mistakes are more likely to result in losses. Let us be clear. In the learning and testing phase of our development, we need to train with the smallest possible trading size in order to safely gain experience and understanding. As we progress, our understanding and execution will become smoother, and our trade results should then reflect the viability and validity of the methods we are applying. Once we notice that we have achieved some competency, we must begin to record our trades so that we can analyze and determine our "trading edge."

Let us assume that we have done 30 trades in various markets using the expanded sideways range pattern. Let us assume that the method produces 16 winning trades and 14 losing trades. The hit rate is then calculated as the ratio of winning trades over total trades. In this case, the hit rate works out to be 0.533. Therefore, the miss rate must be 0.467.

In addition, we can add up all the profits and then find out the average profit per winning trade. We can also add up all the losses and then determine the average loss per losing trade.

Let us say that the average profit per winning trade is $100, and the average loss per losing trade is $60.

This means that based on these numbers, the expanded sideways range pattern has an edge, which can be defined as:

(Average $ Win × by Hit Rate) − (Average $ Loss × by Miss Rate).

This formula is known as the "expectancy," and it defines a very important concept that can objectively measure the statistical reliability of any trading system that is under evaluation.

If we substitute the appropriate numbers into the expectancy formula, we determine that based on these numbers, the method has a positive expectancy, or a winning trading edge of positive 25.28. This number must remain positive for us to succeed over time. The larger the positive expectancy, or winning edge, the better the method is. If this number is negative, then our method is either a long-term losing method, or our execution is flawed. This analysis of the trading method's results will allow us to fine tune our understanding of the market and the execution of our method. Remember, we need to know what to do, then do what we know, and also do it flawlessly.

Let us assume that in our learning and testing phase, we have achieved positive expectancy in the methods we have learned so far. This will mean that over time, the methods that we apply will yield us a positive result.

We are now ready to evolve from the "learning and testing stage" to the "trading for profit" phase.

TRADING FOR PROFITS

In the learning and testing phase, we deliberately traded with the minimum trade size, which will not allow us to make or to lose much! This is because we were focused on the learning process, and are not solely motivated by profit or loss. During this learning phase, we need to hone our understanding of how markets behave, and also polish our execution of our trading methods. Once we are satisfied that we have passed through the learning process, we will now be ready to start applying our knowledge and techniques with the intention of trading for a profitable return.

To do so, we need to be adequately capitalized. Most business ventures fail precisely because they are underfunded and cannot sustain the initial setbacks that can occur. Trading for a living is no different from attempting to succeed in any other business venture.

It is also crucial that we understand that reward always commensurate with the risk we assume. If we wish to make tremendously huge profits with very small capital, then the risk we have to assume must also be very high. This can result in either great pleasure, or great pain!

The winning trader understands this, and is prepared to reduce his rate of return in exchange for a reduced risk of ruin. It is very interesting to note that Warren Buffett's annualized rate of return over the past 50 years averages about 23 percent per annum, so if we can achieve returns above this number consistently over time, we can be justifiably happy with ourselves!

THE PRESERVATION OF CAPITAL

Let us consider this scenario. We have waited patiently for the market to reach a low-risk, high-probability zone, and our method triggers us into a trade. We have a trading capital of $100,000, and we do have a stop loss and a profit exit. For the purpose of this illustration, let us say that should the market reach our profit exit as we anticipate, we stand to amass a profit of $300,000, but should the market shut us out, we stand to lose our entire capital. Literally, this is a make or break scenario, and we cannot afford to be wrong. We cannot even survive one single loss. This is because if we are wrong, we will not have any capital to trade, and therefore will never be able to enjoy potential future profits. As they say, if we wish to win, we must be able to bet, but if we lose all our capital, we cannot bet and therefore cannot win.

Let us now consider the other extreme. With the same capital of $100,000, and the same reward to risk ratio of 3 to 1, we do a trade that will result in a loss of either just $10, or a profit of just $30. Under this scenario, we will be able to survive many losing trades, indeed many consecutive losing trades, but our profits will also be very tiny compared to our trading capital.

MONEY MANAGEMENT: THE PRESERVATION OF OUR CAPITAL

Money management is the art of balancing the need to maximize our return with the fear of losing all our capital. This is a key and crucial component of trading success. All successful traders apply some version of money management. Traders who fail to implement the principles of money management are highly likely to quickly decimate their trading account. The sad fact is that 95 percent of traders fail, and only 5 percent of traders succeed over time.

We have considered two extremes of the money management spectrum. In one scenario, we can lose our entire capital in one single bet; in the other, we can survive numerous consecutive losses, but the bet size does not generate the reward that commensurate with our capital.

Professional fund managers use the fixed fractional ratio at risk principle. Typically, the trading capital is divided into fixed percentages that are then risked in the trade as potential losses. Again, let us consider a trading account with a capital of $100,000 and a fractional risk ratio of 10 percent. This means that in any single trade, the maximum loss that can be endured is $10,000. In martial arts terms, the archer has a quiver with 10 arrows. He then has the ability to accept 10 consecutive misses before his quiver is empty. Now we have a choice. Do we wish to enter combat with a quiver having just 10 arrows, or a quiver containing 50 arrows? Coming back to our hypothetical trading account of $100,000, if we risk $2,000 per trade, we will be able to sustain 50 consecutive losses in a row. The choice of this fixed fractional ratio is solely dependent on our risk profile, our appetite for risk, and also our available capital. Adventurous traders may prefer to risk more in any single trade—not only must these traders have a superior hit rate to succeed over time, they really cannot afford the losses to appear at the start of their trading career. Therein lies the problem that can be called the "probability paradox." On any single open trade, we are never sure whether the end result is going to be a win or a loss. A series of consecutive losses is possible, and more importantly, the distribution of wins and losses can be random.

Many newbie traders may not fully comprehend the potential dangers that lie in wait for the unwary. The newbie trader is most likely to be young and adventurous, but many will eventually learn that the market can and will bite. The few who eventually survive and prosper do so because they have modified their adventurous ways. There will be very few old and experienced adventurous traders, because most of them take on too much risk in their trading and when the law of probability then applies, they are unable to survive the inevitable losses.

Having considered this, we want to preserve our capital and will adopt a conservative approach to money management. We will select 2 percent of capital as the dollar amount of risk in any single trade.

RISK MANAGEMENT COMBINED WITH THE 2 PERCENT MONEY MANAGEMENT RULE

In our study of market behavior and trading setups, we have learned how to determine an entry, and then ensure that we calculate a logical, structural exit for both the stop loss as well as the profit. Deciding the structural risk of any trade will depend on our market understanding. For example, in the expanded sideways range pattern, we expect the market action to be contained within a defined floor and ceiling. We use ATR60 as the filter to systematically define the acceptable variations in the sideways expansion. This is our stop loss, because if the market violates this stop loss, then the expanded sideways range can morph into a directional trend, and if we still hold on to our sideways view, we can be financially killed.

We now need to match the dollar loss of the stop loss to the 2 percent of capital rule. If the structural stop loss results in a loss larger than the stipulated fixed 2 percent, we will not execute the trade. On the other hand, the dollar amount of the structural stop loss may be less than the dollar value of the 2 percent money management rule. In this case, we may be able to assume a larger trade size.

Let us now practice how the money management rule can assist us to decide whether the trade is within our acceptable risk tolerance. Figure 9.1 shows a foreign exchange pair: in this case, the Australian dollar versus the US dollar. Let us assume that our market analysis gives us a buy signal. Our entry price is $0.7844, and our stop loss exit is $0.7562.

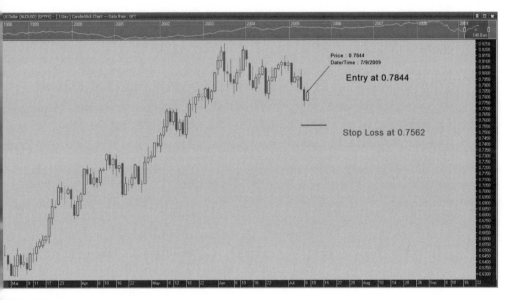

FIGURE 9.1 Initial entry with stop loss
Source: Reproduced by permission of *Market Analyst.*

We need to determine the dollar value of this loss. Perhaps a quick description of FX trading is in order here. FX is the trading of one currency against another. In our example, the Australian dollar

(A$) is traded against the US dollar (US$). The A$ is considered as the principal currency, and the US$ is considered as the secondary currency. Our opinion is that in this case, the trend is up, and we are buying and holding A$, which is the principal currency. We need to use US$0.7844 in order to buy A$1.0000. If we are wrong and the market drops to our stop loss of US$0.7562, the damage to our pocket is US$0.0282. Note that our trade will always be in the principal currency, and the profit and loss will always be expressed in the secondary currency. So now we know the value of the stop loss if we buy a single A$. Obviously, we will not be just trading one single A$. The trading convention is that regular trade size of any principal currency is expressed in integer multiples of 100,000. In other words, the minimum regular trade size is A$100,000, and therefore our loss that we have to plan for will be US$2,820. This is therefore the risk management stop loss that is dictated by our market analysis.

Now let us assume that we have a trading capital of US$50,000, and we have elected 2 percent of our capital as the maximum loss in any given trade. This means that we can only accept trades that have a stop loss risk of US$1000, and therefore even though we believe that the analysis is sound, we cannot take on this A$/US$ trade because we do not have sufficient capital to handle this risk.

The point of this whole exercise is to understand risk and its impact on our trading capital. Remember, if we lose 50 percent of our capital, we will need to make 100 percent of our reduced capital just to break even! Furthermore, if our rate of return is 23 percent per year (what Warren Buffett achieved over the past 50 years), it will take us about four years just to break even. It is important to intellectually understand this concept; more pertinently, we must also emotionally accept the importance of the principle of risk management, because this rule will ensure our financial survival. Staying in the game will allow us to trade safely. This in turn will give us the necessary time to work our superior method of market and trade analysis profitably.

Coming back to our example, can we still trade the A$/US$ with the same stop loss? The short answer is yes, we can. We are relatively fortunate because the FX market is now so large and active, and there are now more service providers who offer the retail trader what is commonly called mini FX contracts. We know that regular trade size in FX is 100,000 of the principal currency. A mini FX contract is in a trade size of 10,000 principal. Therefore, if we now switch to a mini FX service provider, we can determine that the stop loss in a single mini FX contract will cost us US$282. Therefore, we can still take this trade, not on regular size, but in mini contracts.

POSITION SIZING

In the A$/US$ trade that we are looking at, we know that if we trade a single mini FX contract, we will have to be prepared for a loss of US$282. But as we have a capital of $50,000, we can actually risk $1,000 in any given trade. Therefore we can trade more than one single FX mini contract and still be within our predefined rules.

The position sizing formula is to divide the $ amount of the 2 percent rule, by the $ amount of the stop loss based on the minimum trade size. In this case, the $ amount of the 2 percent rule is $1,000, and the $ amount of the stop loss trading one single mini FX, is $282; therefore the allowable position size is 3.5 mini FX contracts. However, FX trading is conducted in integer number of contracts, so we need to *round down* the trade size to just three mini FX contracts.

Let us now apply the same principles to an equity related trade. Figure 9.2 shows Google, a US stock quoted on NASDAQ. What is the analysis and the view that we can derive from this chart?

Can we argue that the uptrend in MA21 has peaked and ended? If so, we can then infer that Google, (the stock) is potentially in a type 1 trend pattern. The current upward move is probably a correction move in a bear market, and we expect the next impulse to trade below the current low shown on this chart.

Based on Figure 9.3, our short entry is at $549.99 per single share and our stop loss is $620.89 per share. Our expected loss is therefore $70.90 for a trade size of a single share.

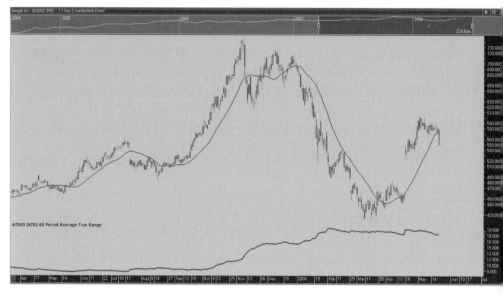

FIGURE 9.2 Equity trade as example
Source: Reproduced by permission of *Market Analyst.*

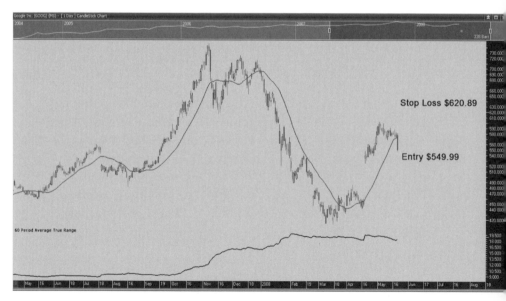

FIGURE 9.3 Equity trade: Entry and stop loss
Source: Reproduced by permission of *Market Analyst.*

The NASDAQ is a regulated stock exchange and like any other regulated exchange, there are rules that govern the conduct of trading activity. One of these rules stipulates that the normal or regular trade size is in multiples of 100 shares. This will mean that if we trade the minimum regular quantity of 100 Google shares, we can expect a potential loss of US$7,090.

Let us now assume that our trading capital is a modest US$30,000. The 2 percent rule will stipulate that any one single trade should not exceed $600 in losses. We can see immediately that the size of our pocket does not match the nature of the risk we have to take, so we cannot trade the regular size of 100 shares.

Fortunately, NASDAQ rules allow for the trading of non-regular quantity, and in the case of Google (the stock) we can trade a minimum of one share. What is the quantity of Google shares we can trade safely? The formula requires us to divide the dollar value of the 2 percent rule (in this example, $600) by the dollar value of the minimum trade quantity (in this example, $70.90). We therefore conclude that we can trade 8.46 shares of Google stock, and this in turn is *rounded down* to eight shares of Google.

WINNING TRADE MANAGEMENT AND THE RULE OF 3

In any given trade, we must be and will be prepared to accept the stop loss if the market does indeed move contrary to our analysis. We have always been stressing this point. It is now time to consider how we need to handle the profitable trade situation. Most traders allow their emotions to rule their trading. When there is profit, the inclination is to quickly realize this profit. Why is this so? Traders are human, and tend to have emotional responses to pleasure and pain. The human psyche tends to gravitate toward pleasure, and will shy away from pain. In trading, profits are pleasurable, so therefore many traders find it easy to quickly take their profit, especially as there is a background fear that the profit may evaporate or even mutate into a loss. How does the human psyche handle the pain of loss? By ignoring it and insidiously hoping that the pain can change into pleasure later! Now this is inevitably a very dangerous pattern, because trading profits will tend to be small, and trading losses will tend to be significantly larger.

We will need to devise a method to manage our natural instincts. We need to have some mechanism to ensure that our losses will be relatively small and affordable, and more importantly, our profits must be significantly larger than our loss. Also, our winning trade management method must allow us to look and feel like a champion trader, at least to ourselves.

The "rule of 3" is one such method. This means that all our trades must be done in sets of at least three minimum contracts. In the example with Google stock, we have determined that we can safely trade eight shares, but the rule of 3 will reduce this to six shares.

What are the exit rules for the rule of 3? The initial rule is known as the break-even rule. We know that our expected loss per share is $70.90. The first exit must give us a profit of twice the expected loss. This means that our expected profit in this case must be set at $141.80, and therefore the first exit level will have to be $141.80 below the entry level, as we are short Google. We can therefore set $408.19 as the first exit level (Figure 9.4).

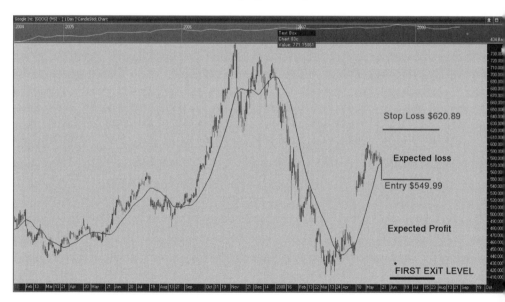

FIGURE 9.4 Trade management: Rule of 3 and the initial break-even exit
Source: Reproduced by permission of *Market Analyst.*

What shall we do when the market gets to the first exit level? We intend to exit one third of the trade position at this first exit. We can quickly see the profit and loss impact by doing the maths:

1. Total initial position size: Sold six Google at $549.99 per share.
2. If the price reaches $408.19 per share, buy exit two Google share.
3. Profit = (2 × $141.80) = $283.60.

Let us now assume that once the first exit level is reached, and we have duly taken our profit, the market does what we do not wish to see. We now assume that the market travels all the way up to our stop loss. What is the impact of this event on our pocket financially? Again, let us do the maths, bearing in mind that we have exited one third of the position size with profit:

1. Total balance position size: Sold four Google shares at $549.99 per share.
2. If the price reaches $620.89 per share, exit four Google shares at stop loss.
3. Loss = (4 × $70.90) = $283.60.

This is clearly a break-even scenario. What we wish to do is to protect and preserve our capital. We need to find and determine the break-even exit price, whereby our initial profit will protect the entire position even if the market shuts us out on the balance of the position. The market eventually reaches our first exit level without us being shut out (Figure 9.5).

There is a very strong psychological reason why we should adhere to this rule. The first reason is that it satisfies the innate desire to put some profit into our pocket. In other words, we need to feel and experience the pleasure of the winning trade. What we have done is to structure this strategy so that the pleasurable exit also conforms to the break-even scenario.

The second reason is that we are now in a stress-free situation whereby we cannot lose any money on this trade. We will be able to

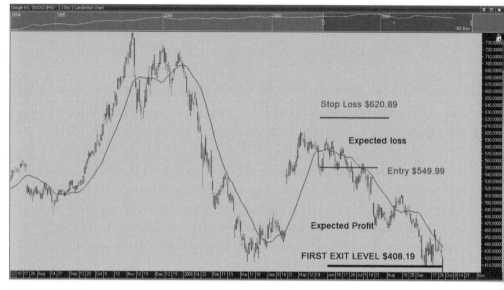

FIGURE 9.5 Exiting at the initial break-even target
Source: Reproduced by permission of *Market Analyst.*

then structure what is now called the core profit exit. This core profit
exit is again derived from our understanding of market behavior, and
because we are in a zero loss situation, we can calmly wait for the
market to give us what we want, and what we want is for the core
profit exit to be achieved. What tool can we use to determine the core
profit exit? We intend to insert the Fibonacci extension to determine a
good quality exit where we believe the impulse may become mature. A
quick refresher is in order at this stage. The original downward move
was an impulse move that changed the previous higher-high, higher-
low uptrend. We will label this impulse as XA. We then waited for the
correction high at B. We initiated a sell trade with the type 1 trend
pattern, and will use the Fibonacci extension method to project the C
exit target from the B high (Figure 9.6).

Notice that the small Fibonacci exit at the 0.618 extension level
is very close to our first exit level. The medium Fibonacci target is
already drawn in the chart, but will be seen in Figure 9.7. We will
place our core profit exit buy order at $268.25, which is the price
level of the medium Fibonacci target for a profit exit.

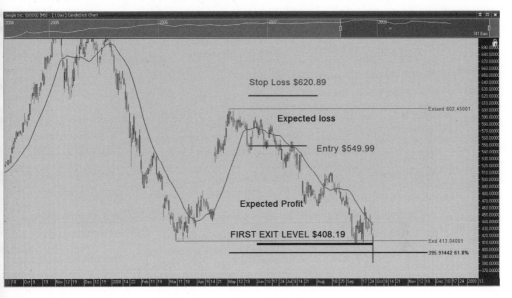

FIGURE 9.6 The core profit exit
Source: Reproduced by permission of *Market Analyst.*

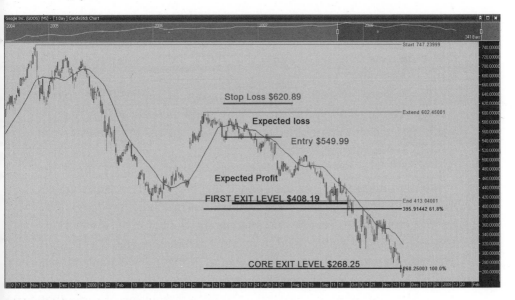

FIGURE 9.7 The core profit exit
Source: Reproduced by permission of *Market Analyst.*

As anticipated by the type 1 trend pattern, the continuation impulse achieved its normal or medium Fibonacci target and we duly exited another one-third of our original position. Let us do the maths to determine our profits:

1. Started with a short position of six Google shares.
2. We bought two Google shares at the first exit level, which resulted in a profit of $283.60. We retain a balance of four Google shares still short.
3. Core profit exit requires us to buy two Google shares at $268.25 in order to partially exit our balance of four Google shares that are still short. Once core profit is realized, we will have a balance of two Google shares still short.
4. Core profit = 2 × ($549.99 − $268.25) = $563.40.
5. Our total profit at this stage will therefore be the sum of the profit from the first exit and the core profit exit. Our profit now stands at $847.

At this stage of our trading campaign, we realize that we still have a short position of two Google shares. We will continue to hold this short position in the hope that the trend in our trading time frame continues.

The rule that we will now apply is to amend our stop loss to our entry price, so that even if the market suddenly and violently goes against us, we should not lose any money on the balance one-third of the original position.

We will now be looking to initiate new positions in the direction of the prevailing trend, as long as we are reasonably confident that the prevailing trend is likely to continue. It is crucially important that we will continue to review and analyze the behavior of this market. This is because we also need to exit the balance of this short trade once we recognize the probability that the trend we wish to see continuing is more than not likely to change.

As the market action continues to unfold, we now observe that the RSI-14 is now accepting above 60. In addition to this observation, we also note that MA21 itself is now in a higher-high, higher-low pattern. This suggests that the downtrend continuation that we expected to see is now less probable. In fact, we need to consider the probability that MA21 is now in a potential uptrend. This in turn means that we may need to *exit all short positions* because the reason to be short is now probably no longer valid.

As we are still short two Google shares at our original entry of $549.99 per share. Exiting now at $401 per share is still profitable (Figure 9.8).

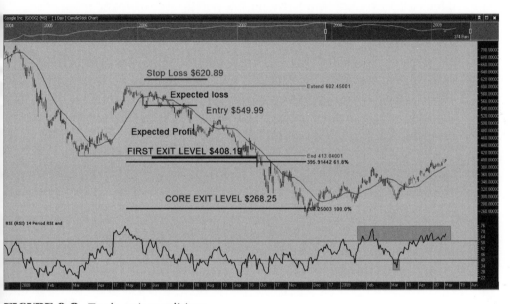

FIGURE 9.8 Trade exit conditions
Source: Reproduced by permission of *Market Analyst.*

Our finalized profit from this Google trade will be the sum of the first exit, the core profit exit, and the final exit.

The key point that we need to understand is that we are trading in sets of three, and at every exit we are reducing our position size by one third. Meanwhile, we are also looking to add new positions (in sets of three) as long as we are reasonably confident that the trend is still in our favor. We will apply the same risk management and trade management rules to any new additional trade. This will allow us to safely build up and pyramid a good winning position.

Perhaps at this stage, it will be proper to discuss how and why most losing traders pyramid their trading positions. More often than not, the trader has taken on a losing position. Let us assume that our typical losing trader has bought XYZ at a price of say $124.18, because his analysis suggests that XYZ can potentially reach $135.15. However, when the market decides to move down, instead of accepting the immediate pain of a stop loss, our typical trader decides to average and pyramid his position at a lower price. At $108.96, he doubles his position, in the hope that if the market goes the way he originally envisages, he can emerge with a reduced loss, or even with a profit. Anyway, if he thinks that $124.18 is a good value for a buy, then at $108.96, XYZ is selling at an even more attractive valuation. In this case, the market continues to slide, and the buy action at both levels now has resulted in a larger loss on the enlarged pyramid position (Figure 9.9).

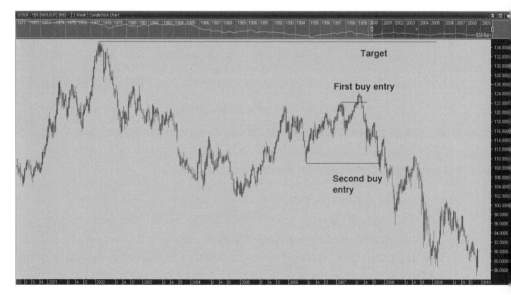

FIGURE 9.9 Never ever average a losing trade
Source: Reproduced by permission of *Market Analyst.*

The trader can only tolerate this loss if his trading is funded strictly by his own capital without any borrowings. In other words, the account is not a margin trading account. The worst that can now occur is that he loses 100 percent of whatever he has invested, should XYZ drop to zero. Should this occur, the financial damage will be indeed painful, but as long as there are zero borrowings, the trader will not be in debt.

The problem that can arise is when our typical trader tries to average a losing position using a highly leveraged margin trading account. Such margin trading accounts can be compared to a double-edged blade; when the trade is correct, the profits are multiplied by the leverage that is employed, but losses are also similarly multiplied and can be financially fatal for our typical trader.

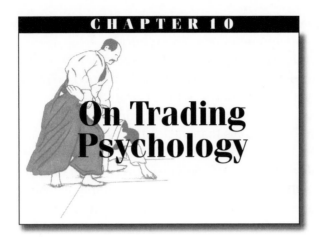

CHAPTER 10

On Trading Psychology

F irstly, I admit that I am not an expert authority on the subject of trading psychology but I can suggest two acknowledged experts in this field. There are also other well-known experts in this specialized field, and the readers are is encouraged to investigate who best suits and fits their personal individual requirements, style, and circumstances.

Dr. Brett Steenbarger has written very some good books on this subject, and also writes a blog that is freely accessible by the general public. Denise Shull is another well-known authority and both Steenbarger and Shull have worked with and helped professional traders successfully.

In his excellent book *The 21 Irrefutable Truths about Trading*, John Hayden provides statistical evidence that 95 percent of traders lose money and only 5 percent of traders are consistent winners over time.

Why is this so? The short answer to this dilemma is that the human psyche tends toward pleasure and shies away from pain. The human psyche also tends toward the yearning wish for instant success with minimum or even no effort.

Unfortunately, the reality is that success requires work.

Those who wish to succeed must find a method to overcome the innate psychological barriers to success.

One key requirement is to clearly define a heartfelt and personally genuine set of goals that will lead to a vision of what success will mean to each of us individually. This is crucial; because without this set of goals and this vision, we can very easily get discouraged by the setbacks and difficulties that will be inevitable whenever we try to master any new activity, and this includes trading.

The process of identifying your own goals and vision can be a difficult process, mainly because this process is emotional in nature, and we need to dig deep within ourselves, in our search for these crucial answers. We may meet unconscious resistance and blocks in this search for our true vision. This is where good professional help may be needed to discover the deeply buried desires of what truly motivates us.

In addition to the vision and goals, it is also crucial to understand how learning takes place. The quickly expanding science of neurology searches for and explains how learning can be significantly hastened. Daniel Coyle's book *The Talent Code* offers great insights to how talent and genius can be grown.

In essence, Coyle discusses a concept called "deep practice," which is effectively a way to break down the required skills into smaller component parts. These parts are practiced, and through correction of mistakes, the component parts of any skill are perfected. These component parts are then strung together into ever more complex tasks and processes. This is very similar to how martial arts skills are transmitted, taught, and learned.

Coyle also mentions the motivation process, which is crucial for the growth of talent and skill. Research has shown that the prefrontal cortex of the human brain requires tremendous amounts of energy to focus on achieving a longer term, distant goal that involves sacrifice, commitment, and even pain. Without this motivation process, the brain will easily default to a much less energy-consuming state where there is no sacrifice, no commitment, and little pain. Obviously, in this state, long-term goals will not be achieved.

There is also the need for a good coach who can assist in the motivation process. A good coach will also be able to transmit and teach good quality, robust methods, and then spot the errors that the student commits in the learning process. By providing feedback and monitoring the correction of mistakes, the good coach can greatly assist the student in accelerating progress toward competency and mastery.

SUMMARY

The core philosophy, beliefs, attitudes, and trading principles of the competent *aiki* trader can be summed up thus:

Beliefs About Success

The winning *aiki* trader must first believe that profits can be made in trading in the markets.

The winning *aiki* trader also believes that he can achieve success in trading.

Most importantly, the winning *aiki* trader knows that he deserves success because of the commitment of his time, his energy, and his resources in honing his skill and abilities.

There are three key technical pillars on which trading success is achieved. It is important to note that all are essential to success, but are not equally weighted.

Market Understanding   This is the pillar that allows us to determine trend and to discover value. The sharpness of our trading plan depends on how well we can master this aspect of success.

1. We need to determine the trend.
2. Then we ask whether the trend is likely to continue or likely to change.

3. The answers to the above questions will determine our stance.

   a. This means that in a continuing uptrend, we are only looking to initiate *buy first* trades.

   b. In a continuing downtrend, we are only looking to initiate *sell first* trades.

   c. In a trend that is at an important support or resistance, the trend may change to *sideways* or even reverse. If our analysis suggests that the trend is likely to change, we can search for *anti-trend* trades.

In other words, the principles of *aikido* are applied here; the trader needs to know the prevailing market force, and be in harmony with this force.

Market understanding also allows us to locate high-probability low-risk action zones and this increases the probability of our success. In an uptrend, we are looking to **buy** undervalued prices. In a downtrend, we are looking to **sell** overvalued prices. Market understanding allows us to put the probabilities of winning **on our side**.

The competent *aiki* trader knows that market understanding comprises only 10 percent of the overall success formula. So although it is a critical component of success, it is by far not the most important.

Risk Management, Money Management, and Trade Management   This is another crucial pillar of success. We ignore or break this rule at our own financial peril. Most casualties of disastrous trading losses come to grief because they have optimistically overestimated the profits without properly considering the risks and whether the risk can be tolerated. Money management and trade management can be expressed as some form of mathematical formulae, so in essence it is simple. But please remember that this set of formulae and rules are designed to increase our chances of survival. We can attribute 30 percent of the overall success formula to risk, money and trade management.

It is also important to realize that risk and money management must work in conjunction with a robust trade plan that demonstrates a winning edge over time. Implementing good risk and money management with a losing trade plan will result in a slowly depleting capital. This is akin to a combatant slowly bleeding away, and this is definitely not the way toward success.

Winning Psychology   Among these three pillars of success, this is the *most important*, with a 60 percent weight in the success formula. In this book, we have been exposed to some of the important concepts and attitudes borrowed from the realm of the martial arts. These borrowed concepts and attitudes will assist us in adopting the habits of success, which will enhance our understanding and practice of winning psychology.

Why is winning psychology so important? If the outer enemy is the market, then the inner enemy is ourselves. It is crucial that we understand our human, emotional responses in trading. Remember, at its most basic and fundamental essence, the human psyche moves toward pleasure and away from pain. The human brain, particularly the prefrontal cortex requires tremendous amounts of energy to overcome inertia, and in the absence of compelling motivation, will prefer not to work! These basic facts have tremendous implications for our trading behavior and also for the way we learn trading.

The trading success formula can be defined as:

$$\text{Trading Success} = (\text{Market Understanding}) \times \\ (\text{Money Management}) \times \\ (\text{Winning Psychology}).$$

Note the multiplication sign. If any one of the three pillars is zero, then trading success will be zero too.

In the learning and practice of martial arts, the beginner is taught specific and very basic patterns. The idea here is to practice these patterns until the execution becomes second nature. Eventually, more complex patterns and techniques can be created by joining various basic patterns and techniques. There is one drawback in such a structured learning process—the student can develop a false sense of confidence and become fixated with his pattern. As they say, a little knowledge can be extremely dangerous! He then tries to "force" a real-life situation to conform to his training pattern. The actual process is to assess whether the real life situation fits the training pattern, and then apply the technique if each scenario matches. The same philosophy should apply to us as practitioners of *aiki* trading. We cannot force the market to fit our patterns or setups that we learn. Instead, we need to assess the market and if the correct market situation presents itself, we can then apply these techniques and trade setups that we have learned. The key is to be able to correctly assess the market, and then correctly select the technique that will allow us a high-probability low-risk entry. We need to remember that such quality opportunities do not occur frequently, so the key to our success is to patiently wait and assess the market for opportunities, and once these quality opportunities arise, strike aggressively! Notice that both patience and decisiveness are key psychological attributes we must cultivate if we desire success in trading, or in martial arts.

One way to also approach trading in the financial markets is to treat market behavior as a dark universe where we as novice traders are stumbling and groping in fear and confusion. Our first response is to acquire knowledge. This knowledge that we acquire will shine a beam of light into this dark universe. We will trade only if we can understand what we see in this cone of light. Market situations that are still in the darkness will be situations that we will elect not to engage in because we are not able to understand it. What we need to do is to gain new knowledge, so that we can increase the size of this beam of light that we now shine into the dark. The stronger the light, the larger will be our area of understanding. This, in turn, will also increase the high-quality, low-risk trade opportunities that we encounter.

This book was written to provide the serious beginner with the initial knowledge so that some light shines into the dark universe of trading. If we persist, practice, and then perfect our understanding and our execution of the concepts discussed here, we will be well placed to continue searching for new sources of light to broaden the visible and understandable part of the market's behavior.

Good luck, and trade well.

Index

A

ACTION, 2

Acceptance, 2, 37, 100, 108, 148

Aiki, 2, 5, 8, 12, 34, 37, 58, 73, 95, 137, 150, 175, 176, 178

Aiki trader, 5, 12, 34, 37, 73, 95, 137, 150, 175, 176

Aikido, 2, 7, 9, 10, 12, 36, 60, 64, 83, 93, 100, 176

Akechi, Mitsuhide, 15, 16

Aikido-ka, 10, 12

Aikijutsu, 8

ATR, 35, 36, 39, 47, 66, 67, 79, 81, 87, 114, 134

Average dollar loss, 45

Average dollar win, 29, 45

Average true range, 35, 36, 66, 79

B

Barros, Ray, xiv

Bearish, 12, 58–60, 62, 78, 87, 93, 101, 103–106, 108, 111, 112, 119, 121, 123, 125, 128, 139, 140, 143, 146, 148, 149, 151

Bears, 28

Bonacci, Leonardo fillius, 71

Breakout, 30–33, 53, 75, 77–79, 81–89, 93, 94, 98, 102, 103, 110–112, 114, 119, 140–153

Breakout momentum, 84–86, 88

Breakout persistency, 86, 88

Breakout power, 81–83, 87, 149, 151

Budo, xi

Buffett, Warren, 156, 160

Bullish, 12, 42, 54, 59, 60, 78, 79, 81, 83, 85, 87, 100–105, 108–113, 132, 139, 140, 143, 145, 146, 149

Bulls, 28, 83

C

Calmness, 3, 69

Candlesticks, 15, 18–21, 54, 75, 83, 113, 123, 125, 139, 140, 149, 150

Capital preservation, 157–158

Chicago Mercantile Exchange, 152

Clarity, 3

Clavell, James, 15

Conner, Dennis, 29

Conner, Laurence A., 29

Contraction, 21, 22, 51, 52, 153

Correction, 5, 21, 23, 28, 51–54, 56–58, 60, 62–64, 66, 68, 72, 77, 87, 94, 97, 98, 100–103, 105, 109–111, 114, 115, 119–121, 123–125, 127–129, 132, 161, 166, 174, 175

Coyle, Daniel, 174

D

Daimyo, 15, 18, 95

Daito, 8

Daito-ryuaikijujutsu, 9

Deep practice, 174

Despair, 3, 20, 35

Directional candles, 21, 125, 140

Divergence, 104, 106–108

Dojima Rice Exchange, 18

Dojo, 2

Down trend, 119

E

Eckhardt, William, 29
Edo, 9
Entry trigger, 32, 33, 66, 67, 88, 103
Expanded sideways pattern, 40–42
Expansion, 21, 22, 31, 34, 51, 52, 97, 98, 127, 128, 135, 153, 158
Exponential moving average, 74, 130

F

Fear, 3, 20, 35, 60, 157, 163, 178
Fibonacci, 71, 72, 119, 120, 124, 125, 127–135, 142, 146, 149, 166, 168
Fibonacci numbers, 71, 72, 119, 120, 142
Fibonacci ratios, 120, 127
FX, 74, 159, 161

G

Goals, 9, 95, 96, 117, 136, 174, 175
Google, 161, 163–165, 169
Gotenjutsu, 8
Greed, 3, 20

H

Harmony, 2, 5, 37, 64, 176
Hayden, John, 35, 173
Hope, 3, 20, 35, 60, 168, 170

I

Imagination, 3–4
Impulse, 21, 23, 28, 29, 51–54, 56–58, 60–64, 66, 68, 69, 72, 77, 94, 98, 100–103, 108–111, 113, 119, 121–125, 127–129, 132, 142, 151, 161, 166, 168

J

Japanese Candlestick Charting Techniques, 19
Jujutsu, 8
Jutsu, 8, 10

K

Kata, 94, 103, 130
Koku, 18

L

Loss, 3, 19, 26, 34–39, 42, 43, 45–47, 60, 66–70, 88–90, 92, 114–116, 125, 126, 134, 135, 143, 144, 154–165, 168, 170, 171

M

Mahjong, 47
Market understanding, 20, 23, 73, 93, 102, 158, 175–177
Market Wizards, 29
McCall, Richard, 2
Miyamoto, Musashi, 96
Money management, 34, 157–159, 176, 177
Munehisa, Honma, 16

N

NASDAQ, 161, 163
Ninja, 95
Nison, Steve, 19

O

Oakes, Lonnie, 4
Obata, Toshishiro, xiv
Oda, Nobunaga, 15, 16
Osaka, 17, 18
OTC, 152
Over-the-counter (OTC), 152

P

Pain, 2, 3, 26, 27, 31, 35, 36, 42, 60, 136, 137, 156, 163, 170, 173–175, 177
Pleasure, 3, 25–27, 31, 35, 42, 60, 136, 137, 156, 163, 165, 173, 177
Position sizing, 161–163
Positive expectancy, 155
Prefrontal cortex, 174, 177
Profit, 3, 25, 27, 29, 35, 37, 38, 40, 42, 43, 45–48, 51, 66, 68–70, 75, 90–92, 114–116, 120, 125–128, 130, 134, 135, 154–156, 158, 160, 163–170

R

Range bound pattern, 23
Raschke, Linda Bradford, 29

Relative Strength Index, 98, 108, 112, 113, 121–123, 125, 132, 133

Resistance, 5, 23, 25, 27, 28, 37, 80, 140–142, 144, 145, 150, 174, 176

Reward, 35, 42–46, 48, 56, 60, 69, 89, 90, 106, 120, 126–128, 130, 134–136, 156, 157

Reward to risk ratio, 43, 45, 46, 48, 56, 90, 135

Risk, 34, 36, 42–46, 48, 56, 60, 68, 69, 75, 78, 89, 90, 95, 116, 120, 126–128, 134, 135, 153, 155–161, 163, 170, 176–178

Risk management, 34, 158, 160, 170, 176

Rule of 3, 163–171

S

Sakata rules, 19

Samurai, 4, 5, 7–9, 17, 18, 48, 98

Schull, Denise, 173

Schwager, Jack, 29

Sengoku jidai, 15

Shinkendo, 4, 7

Shimizu, Seiki

Shogun, 9, 15

Shogunate, 9

Sideways pattern, 23, 25–49, 72, 150, 151

Sideways trend, 5, 29, 46, 51, 54, 61, 62, 72, 74, 87, 93, 94, 97, 103, 108, 119, 125, 142, 150, 153

Simple moving average, 61, 71, 72, 74, 121, 132

Singapore exchange (SGX), 1

Slow stochastic oscillator, 108–117

Steenbarger, Brett, 173

Stop loss, 34–43, 47, 66–68, 70, 88, 89, 114–116, 125, 126, 128, 134, 135, 143, 144, 156, 158–163, 165, 168, 170

Street smarts, 29

Sun Tzu, 9, 75, 150

Support, 5, 23, 25, 27, 28, 140–143, 150, 176

T

Takeda, Sogaku, 8, 9

The Art of War, 19

The Japanese Chart of Charts, 19

The Talent Code, 174

The Twenty One Irrefutable Truths about Trading, 35, 173

The Way of the Warrior Trader, 2

Timeframe, 53, 60–62, 72–75, 78, 87, 100, 102, 104, 105, 120, 121, 123, 130–132, 146, 150, 152, 168

Tokugawa, Ieyasu, 16–18

Toyotomi, Hideyoshi, 16

Trade execution, 71

Trade management, 153–171

Trade plan, 31, 37–39, 42, 69, 88, 90, 92, 115, 116, 134, 177

Trade volume, 139–152

Trust, 3, 46

Turtle soup, 29, 113, 125, 140, 143

Turtles, 28–32, 45, 89

U

Ueshiba, Morihei, 9

Uesugi, Kenshin, 95

Up trend, 108

V

Vision, 85, 95, 117, 174

W

Winning psychology, 177

Wushu, 2

Y

Yodoya, Keian, 17